I0407989

THE ULTIMATE CIVIL RIGHT: EXAMINING THE HYDE AMENDMENT AND THE BORN ALIVE INFANTS PROTECTION ACT

HEARING

BEFORE THE

SUBCOMMITTEE ON THE CONSTITUTION AND CIVIL JUSTICE

OF THE

COMMITTEE ON THE JUDICIARY

HOUSE OF REPRESENTATIVES

ONE HUNDRED FOURTEENTH CONGRESS

SECOND SESSION

SEPTEMBER 23, 2016

Serial No. 114–95

Printed for the use of the Committee on the Judiciary

Available via the World Wide Web: http://judiciary.house.gov

U.S. GOVERNMENT PUBLISHING OFFICE

22–122 PDF   WASHINGTON : 2016

For sale by the Superintendent of Documents, U.S. Government Publishing Office
Internet: bookstore.gpo.gov   Phone: toll free (866) 512–1800; DC area (202) 512–1800
Fax: (202) 512–2104   Mail: Stop IDCC, Washington, DC 20402–0001

COMMITTEE ON THE JUDICIARY

BOB GOODLATTE, Virginia, *Chairman*

F. JAMES SENSENBRENNER, Jr., Wisconsin
LAMAR S. SMITH, Texas
STEVE CHABOT, Ohio
DARRELL E. ISSA, California
J. RANDY FORBES, Virginia
STEVE KING, Iowa
TRENT FRANKS, Arizona
LOUIE GOHMERT, Texas
JIM JORDAN, Ohio
TED POE, Texas
JASON CHAFFETZ, Utah
TOM MARINO, Pennsylvania
TREY GOWDY, South Carolina
RAUL LABRADOR, Idaho
BLAKE FARENTHOLD, Texas
DOUG COLLINS, Georgia
RON DeSANTIS, Florida
MIMI WALTERS, California
KEN BUCK, Colorado
JOHN RATCLIFFE, Texas
DAVE TROTT, Michigan
MIKE BISHOP, Michigan

JOHN CONYERS, Jr., Michigan
JERROLD NADLER, New York
ZOE LOFGREN, California
SHEILA JACKSON LEE, Texas
STEVE COHEN, Tennessee
HENRY C. "HANK" JOHNSON, Jr., Georgia
PEDRO R. PIERLUISI, Puerto Rico
JUDY CHU, California
TED DEUTCH, Florida
LUIS V. GUTIERREZ, Illinois
KAREN BASS, California
CEDRIC RICHMOND, Louisiana
SUZAN DelBENE, Washington
HAKEEM JEFFRIES, New York
DAVID N. CICILLINE, Rhode Island
SCOTT PETERS, California

SHELLEY HUSBAND, *Chief of Staff & General Counsel*
PERRY APELBAUM, *Minority Staff Director & Chief Counsel*

———————

SUBCOMMITTEE ON THE CONSTITUTION AND CIVIL JUSTICE

TRENT FRANKS, Arizona, *Chairman*
RON DeSANTIS, Florida, *Vice-Chairman*

STEVE KING, Iowa
LOUIE GOHMERT, Texas
JIM JORDAN, Ohio

STEVE COHEN, Tennessee
JERROLD NADLER, New York
TED DEUTCH, Florida

PAUL B. TAYLOR, *Chief Counsel*
JAMES J. PARK, *Minority Counsel*

CONTENTS

SEPTEMBER 23, 2016

Page

OPENING STATEMENTS

WITNESSES

LETTERS, STATEMENTS, ETC., SUBMITTED FOR THE HEARING

APPENDIX

MATERIAL SUBMITTED FOR THE HEARING RECORD

OFFICIAL HEARING RECORD

MATERIAL SUBMITTED FOR THE HEARING RECORD BUT NOT REPRINTED

Material submitted by the Honorable Steve Cohen, a Representative in Congress from the State of Tennessee, and Ranking Member, Subcommittee on the Constitution and Civil Justice. This material is available at the Subcommittee and can also be accessed at:

http://docs.house.gov/Committee/Calendar/ByEvent.aspx?EventID=105369

THE ULTIMATE CIVIL RIGHT: EXAMINING THE HYDE AMENDMENT AND THE BORN ALIVE INFANTS PROTECTION ACT

FRIDAY, SEPTEMBER 23, 2016

HOUSE OF REPRESENTATIVES

SUBCOMMITTEE ON THE CONSTITUTION
AND CIVIL JUSTICE

COMMITTEE ON THE JUDICIARY

Washington, DC.

The Subcommittee met, pursuant to call, at 9:10 a.m., in room 2237, Rayburn House Office Building, the Honorable Trent Franks (Chairman of the Subcommittee) presiding.

Present: Representatives Franks, DeSantis, King, Gohmert, Jordan, Cohen, and Conyers.

Also Present: Representative Chu.

Staff Present: (Majority) Paul Taylor, Chief Counsel; Jake Glancy, Clerk; (Minority) Perry Apelbaum, Staff Director & Chief Counsel; James Park, Minority Counsel; Matthew Morgan, Professional Staff Member; and Veronica Eligan, Professional Staff Member.

Mr. FRANKS. Good morning. The Subcommittee on the Constitution and Civil Justice will come to order. And, without objection, the Chair is authorized to declare recesses of the Committee at any time.

We welcome everyone today to this hearing. We are calling it "The Ultimate Civil Right: Examining the Hyde Amendment and the Born-Alive Abortion Survivors Protection Act." And I would now recognize myself for an opening statement.

Today, we will hear testimony on existing statutory language prohibiting taxpayer funding from paying for the taking of the lives of pre-born children through abortion. There is concern that the Obama administration or a potential Clinton administration may intend to reinterpret the plain and longstanding meaning of the Hyde amendment. We will also examine today the Born-Alive Abortion Survivors Protection Act, which would protect human babies who are born alive.

On this day in the year 2016 in the land of the free and the home of the brave, there are no criminal penalties in Federal law for either negligently or deliberately killing born alive human babies who are living and breathing on the table after surviving an abortion.

(1)

More than 7 months ago, the U.S. House of Representatives passed the Born-Alive Abortion Survivors Protection Act, with bipartisan support, to protect these little children who are born alive. More than 90 percent of the American people support this kind of legislation, yet we have been unable to even get a vote or even a debate in the United States Senate to protect innocent born-alive babies from being deliberately subjected to cruel and torturous death.

The people who came upon Kermit Gosnell's clinic in Philadelphia and discovered a horrifying scene and several dead babies, many of whom had been born alive before being murdered, were told by their supervisor that the investigation of abortion was not their business. This insidious sense has taken hold that if we are dealing with abortion and any of its aspects, we were dealing with a ''constitutional right'' which overrode or trumped any local law that might protect the victims.

Ashley Baldwin, one of Dr. Gosnell's clinic employees, said she saw babies breathing and she described one as 2 feet long that no longer had eyes or mouth, but in her words, was making like this screeching noise. It sounded like a little alien.

The abortion industry has labored for all of these decades to convince the world that unborn children and born children should be completely separated in our minds, that while born children are persons worthy of protection, unborn children are not persons and are not worthy of protection. But those who now oppose this bill to protect born-alive children suddenly have the impossible task of convincing themselves and the American people that a born-alive premature baby that has survived an abortion is just a fetus that should be disposed of and not a little human baby, not a little human child worthy of our protection as a Nation.

To any compassionate human being who has not invincibly hardened his or her heart or soul, an honest consideration of this absurd inconsistency is profoundly enlightening.

I would earnestly implore in this moment in this Committee that the majority leader of the United States Senate, and I say this in the most personal of terms, asking him to hold in some form a recorded vote on the Born-Alive Abortion Survivors Protection Act in the U.S. Senate to provide criminal penalties at the Federal level to prevent monsters like Kermit Gosnell from murdering innocent born-alive human babies.

Now, President Obama vetoed similar legislation—voted against, forgive me—President Obama voted against similar legislation four times before becoming President, and astonishingly now has promised in writing to veto this bill if it comes to his desk. And I am told Mrs. Clinton holds the same position but intends at all costs to avoid revealing that during the Presidential campaign.

Ladies and gentlemen, this is not abortion. This is born alive. Born alive. The American people deserve to know where candidates for President stand on something so foundationally intrinsic to the Republic founded on these core principles that all of us are created equal and are children of God.

The American people still deeply hold themselves to be protective of born children, and if those seeking the highest office in the land are in opposition to a bill that would protect born-alive children, then the American people have a right to know this before the most important election in this century, and in the last century, on which the core right to live contained in the Constitution of the United States itself hangs in the balance.

Turning our backs on helpless born-alive children is not who we are as a people, and it is not who the United States of America has become as a Nation. Yet it is one of the most crucial questions now upon us in this divisive moment in history, in this decisive moment of history as well, and the implication for this country's soul and future are profound beyond words.

And so I thank the witnesses for being here, and I ask this morning that all of us just open our hearts to the truth.

And I would now recognize the Ranking Member, Mr. Cohen for 5 minutes.

Mr. COHEN. Thank you, Mr. Chair.

It is undisputed that the Constitution guarantees women in this country what I believe is the most fundamental and personal decision they will ever make about their reproductive health—whether or not to have children—and the Supreme Court made that clear in 1973 in *Roe v. Wade*. The Court has repeatedly reaffirmed the Constitution's guarantee of this right, most recently, in June in *Whole Woman's Health Clinic v. Hellerstedt.*

There are people, like Mr. Franks and myself, who have strong opinions on the issue and diametrically opposed positions, and we will not change each other's minds today or tomorrow or probably ever.

So why are we here today when the House of Representatives is in recess?

One week from today marks the 40th anniversary of the Hyde amendment, and the Hyde amendment is a rider that is attached to appropriations bills that fund the Department of Health and Human Services. It bans Federal funding for abortion services provided by Medicaid and other Health and Human Services programs, with limited exceptions, and that was hard fought, for mothers' lives or in the case of rape or incest. Medicaid, of course, is the primary public health insurance program for low-income Americans.

And this makes me think back to a program I attended last Friday night where Gloria Steinem spoke. And Gloria Steinem spoke about the fact that controlling women's reproductive processes has been something that men have done for years, and tried to do, and they have tried to control women and they have tried to control people of different races and people of different sexual orientations, because they liked the power they had and they wanted to keep it that way.

And women, in the days of slavery, were very much encouraged to have children, because that was good, because you needed lots of more property to bring the crops to make the money. Then when they came along with the mechanization, they didn't need so many people, they started to think less of having children. But it was the people at the top, the people that owned the land and had the controls, determined a lot and wanted to continue to control women's reproductive systems.

Poor women experience five times the rate of unintended pregnancies than more affluent women—five times more—with abortion becoming more and more concentrated among low-income women as a result. And women of color are disproportionately likely to be poor and rely on Medicaid for health services, health insurance, and this racial disparity is particularly true among women of reproductive age.

Therefore, the Hyde amendment, when you really look at what it does, it bans the funding for abortion services through Medicaid, denying low-income and minority women the ability to access a safe and legal reproductive health service.

Perhaps the late Supreme Court Justice Thurgood Marshall, one of the greatest men to ever serve on the Supreme Court, put it most succinctly when he wrote in 1980 that the Hyde amendment is designed to deprive poor and minority women of the constitutional right to choose, because that, in effect, is what it does.

Simply put, the opponents to the right to choose cannot get what they really want, which is to repeal *Roe* outright, so instead they have chosen to deny the right, as a practical matter, to poor women and women of color.

Most Americans, whatever their views on the right to choose, agree that politicians should not be allowed to deny a woman health insurance coverage for pregnancy-related care just because she is poor, and this includes coverage for abortion services. The right to choose is well settled, and the amount of money a woman has should not determine whether she could exercise her fundamental constitutional right.

You know, before *Roe v. Wade*, wealthy women could make their ways to Canada or Mexico, and they could get abortions, but poor women couldn't. Money has always been a factor.

I am a cosponsor of H.R. 2972, the ''EACH Woman Act of 2015,'' introduced by the dynamic and great leader, Representative Barbara Lee, who is in the audience and who has a statement, which with the permission of the Chair, I would like to introduce and make part of the record, without exception.

Mr. FRANKS. Without objection.

[The information referred to follows:]

United States House of Representatives Committee on the Judiciary
Subcommittee on the Constitution and Civil Justice

Hearing: "The Ultimate Civil Right: Examining the Hyde Amendment and the Born Alive Infants Protection Act"

Written Testimony of Congresswoman Barbara Lee
September 23, 2016

Mr. Chairman and Distinguished Members of this Subcommittee:

Thank you for the opportunity to submit written testimony regarding the harmful and shameful Hyde Amendment.

Next week marks forty years since the Hyde Amendment was first passed here in Congress. Forty years ago, I was one of only a handful of young women of color working on Capitol Hill. Just a few years earlier, the Supreme Court affirmed a woman's right to a legal abortion with the *Roe v. Wade* decision. I was hopeful that our country was starting a new chapter, an era of respect for women's reproductive healthcare decisions.

Just months after the decision though, Senator Jesse Helms began working to chip away at women's access to their constitutional right to safe and legal abortion. He worked in the Senate to pass a constitutional amendment to ban abortion, and he collaborated with Congressman Henry Hyde in the House to find a new way to undermine women's reproductive rights through the appropriations process.

In September 1976, we fought tooth and nail to prevent the Hyde Amendment from being included in the 1977 federal spending bill. But ideologically driven politicians, convinced that THEY knew what was best for women, were successful in denying abortion coverage for women enrolled in Medicaid.

Little did we know that this harmful rider would help pave the way for decades of harsh, unfair restrictions on abortion rights. Over the years, the pain and punishment of the Hyde Amendment has been extended to deny coverage to federal employees and their dependents, military service members, Native Americans, Peace Corps volunteers, immigrants, federal prisoners, and residents of Washington, D.C.

Just since 2010, state legislatures have adopted 334 abortion restrictions, further expanding the hardship of abortion coverage bans like the Hyde Amendment. From shutting down clinics to creating longer wait times, these restrictions impose the greatest burden on low-income people, immigrants, women of color, and young people.

The number of women potentially affected by the Hyde Amendment is enormous. Of women aged 15–44 enrolled in Medicaid, 60% live in the 35 states and the District of Columbia that do not cover abortion, except in limited circumstances. This amounts to roughly seven million women of reproductive age, including 3.4 million who are living below the federal poverty level (FPL).

More than half of the women subject to the Hyde Amendment are women of color. Thirty percent of black women and 24% of Hispanic women aged 15–44 are enrolled in Medicaid, compared with 14% of white women.

We also know that a woman who wants to get an abortion, but is denied, is more likely to fall into poverty than a woman who is able to access one.

Let me be clear. Regardless of her zip code, her employer, or her income, women should have EQUAL access to the full range of reproductive health services, including abortion.

That's why I, along with seventy of my colleagues, introduced the EACH Woman Act (H.R. 2972) last July. This legislation would lift the coverage bans that prevent women from making the decision that is best for her and her family.

Today, we have more than 120 cosponsors working to stop politicians from interfering with a woman's reproductive rights. As Members of Congress, we should be empowering people to make the decisions best for their lives, NOT enacting more restrictions.

But this movement isn't just Members of Congress, it's people and organizations of conscience including abortion funds, providers, labor unions, people of faith, Black, Latino, and Asian American communities, and youth organizations have declared their support.

Together, we will continue to work to END the Hyde Amendment and similar coverage restrictions to ensure equal access to abortion services for ALL women. I am committed to working with this committee and community partners to achieve our bold vision of reproductive justice for everyone.

Mr. COHEN. That, too.

I thank you for being here. And thank you for all you have done. When I was with Ms. Steinem, I asked her about her heroes, and you and Maxine Waters were right there among them.

This bill, which Representative Lee has sponsored, would ensure, among other things, that Federally funded medical coverage extends to all pregnancy-related healthcare services, including abortion services. The unjust burdens that the Hyde amendment has imposed on low-income and minority women demand that Congress pass H.R. 2972.

Mr. Franks, I don't know the poll, and I know that you can have polls of all kind of natures. I don't know if 90 percent of the people support this and how it was phrased. But I do know that about 90 percent of the people support no fly, no buy, and we can't get a vote on that in the House. And if you take some guns from people who are considered too dangerous to fly, you will save some people's lives for sure, people who are here today, but we don't do it.

It is time to rescind the Hyde amendment and guarantee that all women are able to access quality reproductive healthcare services and exercise their constitutional rights without regard to their socioeconomic status.

I yield back the balance of my time.

Mr. FRANKS. And I thank the gentleman.

And I would now recognize the full Committee Ranking Member, Mr. Conyers of Michigan, for his opening statement.

Mr. CONYERS. Thank you, Mr. Chairman, and I welcome the witnesses for today's important hearing.

In *Roe v. Wade*, the Supreme Court recognized a woman's constitutional right to make what is perhaps the most personal of healthcare decisions—when to start a family—free from undue government interference.

Unfortunately, though, since 1976, Congress has sought to undermine this important constitutional right by attaching the so-called Hyde amendment to annual appropriation measures funding the Department of Health and Human Services. The Hyde amendment, of course, is named after a former colleague on the Judiciary Committee, Chairman Henry Hyde, which prohibits the use of Federal Medicaid funds to pay for an abortion except to protect the mother's life or in cases of rape or incest.

There are many reasons why this restriction should be rescinded. To begin with, the Hyde amendment is a blatant example of political decisionmaking inappropriately interfering in women's healthcare decisions. For more than 40 years, *Roe v. Wade* has been the law of the land, as has been indicated, yet it is clear that the Hyde amendment's purpose is to undermine the *Roe v. Wade* constitutional guarantee of a right to choose to terminate a pregnancy by limiting low-income women's access to safe, legal medical care.

Political people, elected officials, most of whom are not doctors, have little or no business interfering in a woman's constitutionally protected private healthcare decisions in order to impose their own views about women's rights in health care.

In addition, the Hyde amendment has a disproportionately detrimental effect on the health of low-income women and the well-being of their families. According to the Guttmacher Institute, many low-income women lacking medical coverage are forced to delay paying their utility bills, rent, groceries even, for themselves or their children, to seek out financial assistance from relatives or friends, or to sell personal belongings in order to pay for an abortion.

Moreover, women who cannot afford abortion procedures may, in desperation, resort to self-inducing an abortion or turn to unsafe, untrained, unlicensed practitioners, heightening the risk of injury or death from what is supposed to be a safe and legal medical procedure.

Finally, the Hyde amendment disproportionately affects women of color, which has been indicated. Medicaid provides medical coverage to 20 percent of women of reproductive age, but as a result of social and economic inequality tied to the persistence of racism in our society, 30 percent of African American women and 20 percent of Hispanic women of reproductive age are enrolled in Medicaid compared to just 14 percent of White women of reproductive age. Clearly, the consequences of the Hyde amendment disproportionately fall on women of color.

While 15 States permit the use of their own funds to provide abortion coverage for Medicaid enrollees, 60 percent of reproductive age women enrolled in Medicaid live in States that only cover abortion in limited circumstances. Rather than undermine the constitutional right of low-income women and women of color, Congress should look to these States as an example and act to ensure that women, regardless of their financial situation, have access to quality comprehensive reproductive health services.

And so I am going to carefully listen to the testimony that comes forth, and I thank the witnesses for being with us today.

And I yield back, Mr. Chairman.

Mr. FRANKS. And I thank the gentleman.

I will now introduce our witnesses. Our first witness is Ms. Giana Jessen. Ms. Jessen is an abortion survivor. Our second witness is Ms. Genevieve Plaster. Ms. Plaster is the senior policy analyst at the Charlotte Lozier Institute. Our third witness is Ms. Kierra Johnson. Mr. Johnson is the executive director at the organization URGE. Our fourth and final witness is Ms. Arina Grossu. Ms. Grossu is the director for the Center for Human Dignity at the Family Research Council.

Now, each of the witnesses' written statements will be entered into the record in its entirety, and I would ask that each witness summarize her testimony in 5 minutes or less. To help you stay within that time, there is a timing light in front of you. The light will switch from green to yellow indicating that you have 1 minute to conclude your testimony. When the light turns red, it indicates that the witness' 5 minutes have expired.

And before I recognize the witnesses, it is the tradition of the Subcommittee that they be sworn. So if you would please stand to be sworn.

Do you swear that the testimony you are about to give before this Committee is the truth, the whole truth, and nothing but the truth, so help you God?

You may be seated.

Let the record reflect that all of the witnesses responded in the affirmative.

And I would now recognize our first witness, Ms. Giana Jessen.

And if you would please turn that microphone on before you speak. Pull it there close.

Ms. JESSEN. Okay. Can you hear me?

Mr. FRANKS. Yes, ma'am.

TESTIMONY OF GIANA JESSEN, ABORTION SURVIVOR

Mr. JESSEN. Pardon me. Thank you. Thank you very much for giving me the opportunity to speak with you this morning.

I wish to appeal not only to those present within this chamber today, but to my Nation. We are here to discuss infanticide. I am greatly troubled that this hearing is even necessary and that such a law to prevent infanticide must be constructed in the United States of America at all.

Many Americans have no idea that babies can even live through abortions and are often left to die, but this does happen. I know this because I was born alive in an abortion clinic after being burned in my mother's womb for 18 hours. My medical records clearly state the following: Born during saline abortion/April 6, 1977/6 a.m./2½ pounds. Triumphantly, I entered this world. I added that part.

Apart from Jesus himself, the only reason I am alive is the fact that the abortionist had not yet arrived at work that morning. Had he been there, he would have ended my life by strangulation, suffocation, or simply leaving me there to die.

Instead, I lived and have the gift of cerebral palsy as a direct result of lack of oxygen to my brain while surviving an abortion. And cerebral palsy, make no mistake, is a tremendous gift. I don't know if any of you understand, maybe you do, what a tremendous honor it is to have to lean on the strong arm of Jesus all the way to heaven. It is my honor, in a country that doesn't wish to speak his name, I will.

So by the grace of God, in my case, a nurse called an ambulance and had me transferred to a hospital. That nurse saved my life, and I am profoundly grateful to her for this.

Those who wish to justify such unspeakable evil, such as leaving a baby without proper medical care to die, have become masters of the manipulation of language, intimidation, and defaming their opponents to achieve their wicked aims. As a Nation, we are continuously exchanging the truth for a lie. We have neglected our soul. And what will it take for us to awaken from our numbness and indifference regarding this? Will we ever awake?

I am confounded as well by the passivity so often demonstrated by otherwise good and just men, by the fact that we must plead with those in power to give the most vulnerable infants among us even one moment of their attention.

This is a bipartisan issue, and I think it is important for the American people to weigh at this hour whether or not they wish to elect someone to the highest office in the land that favors infanticide, because that is what we are speaking of here, a child, exactly as I was, that had the audacity to live through her mother's abortion and needed immediate and proper care.

So I would like to ask Mr. Trump to tell me, and you, where he specifically stands on this issue, and I would ask the same of Mrs. Clinton. I would also ask Senator Mitch McConnell to force a vote on the Born-Alive Abortion Survivors Protection Act before the end of this September.

I have faced the consequences of our choices as a Nation, as evidenced by my cerebral palsy. So if you choose to do nothing, I believe I at least deserve to know why you find this abhorrent practice tolerable, and I would respectfully, respectfully ask that you tell me directly.

It seems in some ways we have lost our way in this beautiful Nation. But it needn't be so. We have only to remember that we are lent each breath, that we are all engraved upon the hands of God, and therefore cannot for one single moment be forgotten by him. We need only to remember Jesus, who took me from my mother's womb to be his own.

Thank you.

[The testimony of Ms. Jessen follows:]

Prepared Statement of Gianna Jessen, Abortion Survivor

Thank you very much for giving me the opportunity to speak with you this morning.

I wish to appeal not only to those present within this chamber today, but to my nation.

We are here to discuss infanticide. I am greatly troubled that this hearing is even necessary, and that such a law to prevent infanticide must be constructed in the United States of America at all.

Many Americans have no idea that babies can even live through abortions and are often left to die. But this does happen.
I know this because i was born alive in an abortion clinic after being burned in my mother's womb for 18 hours.

My medical records clearly state the following: Born during saline abortion/April 6, 1977/6am/ 2/1/2 pounds.

Apart from Jesus himself, the only reason I am alive is the fact that the abortionist had not yet arrived at work that morning. Had he been there, he would have ended my life by strangulation, suffocation or simply leaving me there to die.

Instead, I lived and have the gift of cerebral palsy as a direct result of lack of oxygen to my brain while surviving an abortion.

By the grace of God, in my case, a nurse called an ambulance and had me transferred to a hospital. That nurse saved my life and I am profoundly grateful to her for this.

Those who wish to justify such unspeakable evil, such as leaving a baby without proper medical care to die, have become masters of the manipulation of language, intimidation and defaming their opponents to achieve their wicked aims.

As a nation, we are continuously exchanging the truth for a lie. We have neglected our soul. What will it take for us to awaken from our numbness and indifference regarding this? Will we ever wake?

I am confounded as well by the passivity so often demonstrated by otherwise good and just men; by the fact that we must plead with those in power to give the most vulnerable infants among us, even one moment of their attention.

This is a bipartisan issue, and I think it's important for the American people to weigh at this hour, whether or not they wish to elect someone to the highest office in the land that favors infanticide. Because that is what we are speaking of here, a child, exactly as I was, that had the audacity to live through her mother's abortion and needed immediate and proper care.

So I would like to ask Mr. Trump to tell me, and you, where he specifically stands on this issue, and I ask the same of Mrs. Clinton.

I would also like to ask Senator Mitch McConnell to force a vote on the Born Alive Abortion Survivors Protection Act before the end of this September.

I have faced the consequences of our choices as a nation (as evidenced by my Cerebral Palsy.) So if you choose to do nothing, I believe I at least deserve to know why you find this abhorrent practice tolerable, and i would respectfully ask that you tell me directly.

It seems in some ways, we have lost our way in this beautiful nation. But it needn't be so. We have only to remember that we are lent each breath, that we are all engraved upon the hands of God, and therefore, cannot for a single moment, be forgotten by him. We need only to remember Jesus, who took me from my mothers womb, to be his own.

Thank you.

———

Mr. FRANKS. Thank you, Ms. Jessen.

And I would now recognize our second witness, Ms. Plaster.

And if you would turn on your microphone, please.

TESTIMONY OF GENEVIEVE PLASTER, M.A., SENIOR POLICY ANALYST, CHARLOTTE LOZIER INSTITUTE

Ms. PLASTER. Chairman Franks, Ranking Member Cohen, and distinguished Members of the Subcommittee, thank you for inviting me to testify before your Subcommittee during this hearing on "The Ultimate Civil Right: Examining the Hyde Amendment and Born Alive Infants Protection Act." My name is Genevieve Plaster, and I am a senior policy analyst for the Charlotte Lozier Institute, a research and education resource in Washington, D.C.

Today, I will focus on the Hyde amendment and its measurable impact over the past 40 years. The Hyde amendment is an appropriations rider that prohibits the use of Federal funds for elective abortion or for health benefits that cover elective abortion. As a rider, it is not a permanent law, but it has been passed with bipartisan support in every Federal funding bill since 1976.

Amidst legal challenges in its early years, the Hyde amendment was reaffirmed as constitutional in 1980 by the U.S. Supreme Court in *Harris v. McCrae.* Though a financial policy, the most important measurement of the Hyde Amendment's real world effects has not been dollars saved but lives saved. By saying that the Hyde amendment has saved lives, I am referring to the prevented abortions due to women deciding to continue their pregnancies and give birth to their children in the absence of Federal funding.

More than 20 peer-reviewed studies published in academic journals have found a reduction in abortion rates following the enactment of the Hyde amendment or other similar laws. Numerous studies also examining State data show not only the abortion rate decreased, but that the birth rate has increased.

In fact, the Guttmacher Institute, formerly Planned Parenthood's research arm, which in prior years received millions of funding from the business after still splitting with them, conducted its own literature review on the impact of the Hyde amendment on abortion rates in 2009. Because the decline in abortion was so clear, even the study's authors were forced to acknowledge that the "best studies found 18 to 37 percent of pregnancies that would have ended in Medicaid-funded abortion were carried to term when public funding was no longer available." We then rightly acknowledge that the Medicaid-funded births of these individuals are lives saved due to the Hyde amendment.

In a forthcoming study, the Charlotte Lozier Institute's associate scholar, Dr. Michael New, calculates the best estimate for how many lives have been saved by the Hyde amendment. With a rigorous methodology, Dr. New identified solid appropriately designed studies that examine the decrease of abortion rates following the enactment of a public funding limitation.

Finding the average of decrease to be 1.52, he applies this rate to State-specific data, namely the number of years and months that each State has had the implementation, as well as each State's abortion rate.

The study's major conclusion is that the Hyde amendment has saved more than 2 million lives since 1976, 2 million Americans. That is approximately the entire population of the city of Houston, the fourth-largest city in the U.S. Two million Americans is the entire population of the State of New Mexico.

From another angle, the study also calculated that the Hyde amendment saves approximately 60,000 lives each year. Among just the seven States that each of you and your constituents call home, the Hyde amendment has saved approximately 700,000 lives since its enactment. That is, in Arizona, 55,000 lives were saved; in Florida, 166,000; in Iowa, 33,000; in Ohio, 131,000; in Tennessee, 66,000; in Texas, the highest number of lives saved at nearly a quarter million, 248,000. And finally in New York, regretfully, no lives have been saved due to the Hyde amendment because the State has had State-funded abortion since 1976 till today.

This real world impact bears repeating. In just these seven States represented, 700,000 lives have been saved by the Hyde amendment.

From another perspective, CLI scholar Dr. New explains that we can also say one in nine people born under Medicaid in a State that does not have a Medicaid-funded abortion program was saved thanks to the Hyde amendment.

Lest we lose sight of the qualitative reality of 2 million lives, let us consider a brief story of Claire, a young woman who experienced an unplanned pregnancy at age 17. In a recent news article that was just published the other week, she said that at that time, ''I felt hopeless and alone.'' She explained that if Medicaid funding for an abortion had been available to her, it would have been very tempting to go ahead and have that abortion.

Instead, she reached out for support, was accompanied to a pregnancy care center, where she saw the first ultrasound of her young son, and decided to continue this pregnancy. Now, a year later, Claire reflects, ''I don't know what I would do without him. That is my baby.''

Of the 2 million lives saved by the Hyde amendment, one can only wonder how many other of the mothers were in a similar situation.

In conclusion, the Hyde amendment has enjoyed bipartisan support for 40 years, was reaffirmed as constitutional in 1980, enjoys support from nearly 7 in 10 Americans, including even 51 percent of those who identify as pro-choice, 44 percent of those who are Democrats, 65 percent of African Americans, 61 percent of Latinos, and finally and most importantly, has saved an estimated 2 million lives.

For these compelling reasons, the protective language of the Hyde amendment should not only be retained as enforced policy but should also be codified as permanent law.

Thank you for inviting me to testify today.

[The testimony of Ms. Plaster follows:]

Written Testimony of Genevieve Plaster, M.A.
Senior Policy Analyst, Charlotte Lozier Institute

Hearing of the U.S. House Judiciary Committee,

Subcommittee on the Constitution and Civil Justice

Regarding "The Ultimate Civil Right: Examining the Hyde Amendment
and the Born Alive Infants Protection Act"

September 23, 2016
9:00 a.m.
2237 Rayburn Building

Hon. Trent Franks, Chair

Hon. Steve Cohen, Ranking Member

Honorable Members

United States House of Representatives

Committee on the Judiciary

Subcommittee on the Constitution and Civil Justice

2237 Rayburn House Office Building

Washington, DC 20515-6216

Chairman Franks, Ranking Member Cohen, and Distinguished Members of the Subcommittee:

Thank you for inviting me to testify before your subcommittee during this hearing on "The Ultimate Civil Right: Examining the Hyde Amendment and Born Alive Infants Protection Act."

My name is Genevieve Plaster, and I am a senior policy analyst for the Charlotte Lozier Institute, a research and education resource in Washington, D.C. Today, I will focus on the Hyde Amendment and its measurable impact over the past 40 years.

Background

The Hyde Amendment is an appropriations rider that prohibits the use of federal funds for elective abortion or for health benefits coverage that includes elective abortion.[1] As a rider, it is not a permanent law, but it has been passed with bipartisan support in every federal funding bill since 1976. Amidst legal challenges in its early years, the Hyde Amendment was re-affirmed as constitutional in 1980 by the U.S. Supreme Court in *Harris v. McCrae*.[2]

Though a financial policy, the most important measurement of the Hyde Amendment's real-world effects has not been dollars saved, but lives saved.

By saying the Hyde Amendment has "saved lives," I am referring to the prevented abortions due to women deciding to continue their pregnancies and give birth to their children in the absence of public funding. More than 20 peer-reviewed studies published in academic journals have found a reduction in abortion rates following the enactment of the Hyde Amendment or other laws that limit public funding of abortion. Numerous studies examining state data show not only the abortion rate reduction, but also an increased birthrate. In fact, the Guttmacher Institute – formerly Planned Parenthood's research arm which still received millions of dollars from the

---

[1] Consolidated Appropriations Act, 2016, Division H, Title V, Sec 506 to 507 (c), accessed at: http://docs.house.gov/billsthisweek/20151214/CPRT-114-HPRT-RU00-SAHR2029-AMNTlfinal.pdf

[2] *Harris v. McRae*, 448 U.S. 297 (1980)

abortion business after splitting – conducted its own literature review on the impact of the Hyde Amendment on abortion rates in 2009. Because the decline in abortion was so clear, even the study's authors were forced to acknowledge that the "best studies…found that 18-37 percent of pregnancies *that would have ended in Medicaid-funded abortion were carried to term* when funding was no longer available."[3] (Emphasis mine) We then rightly acknowledge that the Medicaid-funded births of these children (though the oldest are now 40 years old) are "lives saved" due to the Hyde Amendment.

Quantitative Impact of the Hyde Amendment

In a forthcoming study, Charlotte Lozier Institute associate scholar, Dr. Michael J. New, calculates the best estimate for how many lives have been saved by the Hyde Amendment. With a rigorous methodology, Dr. New identifies solid, appropriately designed studies that examine the decrease of abortion rates following the enactment of a public funding limitation. Finding the average rate of decrease to be 1.52, he then applies this rate to state-specific data – namely, the number of years and months each state has had an implemented Medicaid funding limitation for abortion, as well as each state's abortion rate.

The major conclusion of this groundbreaking study is that the **Hyde Amendment has saved more than two million lives since 1976.** Two million Americans – that's approximately the entire population of the city of Houston, the 4th largest city in the U.S.[4]; two million Americans is the entire population of the state of New Mexico[5]; two million Americans is the sum of the entire combined populations of Rhode Island[6] and Delaware[7].

From another angle, the study also calculated that the **Hyde Amendment saves approximately 60,000 lives each year.**

Among just the seven states that each of you and your constituents call home, the Hyde Amendment has saved approximately 700,000 lives since its enactment. That is, in:

- Arizona – 55,000 lives were saved;
- Florida – 166,000;
- Iowa – 33,000;
- Ohio – 131,000;
- Tennessee – 66,000;
- Texas – highest number of lives saved at more than a quarter million (248,000); and finally in
- New York – regretfully, no lives have been saved due to the Hyde Amendment since the state has had state Medicaid-funded abortion from 1976 to 2015.

---

[3] Henshaw SK *et al.* Restrictions on Medicaid Funding for Abortions: A Literature Review, Guttmacher Institute. June 2009, accessed at: https://www.guttmacher.org/sites/default/files/report_pdf/medicaidlitreview.pdf
[4] http://www.census.gov/quickfacts/table/PST045215/4835000,00
[5] http://www.census.gov/quickfacts/table/PST045215/35,4835000,00
[6] http://www.census.gov/quickfacts/table/PST045215/44,35,4835000,00
[7] http://www.census.gov/quickfacts/table/PST045215/44,35,4835000,00

This real-world impact bears repeating: In just these seven states, 700,000 Americans have been saved by the Hyde Amendment.

From another perspective, CLI scholar Dr. New explains that we can also say **one in nine lives was saved thanks to the Hyde Amendment**. In three separate studies examining Illinois, Ohio, and Texas, the state's Medicaid-birthrates increased after implementation of the Hyde Amendment by an average of 12.8 percent. If, hypothetically, there were 100 babies born while abortion was still funded under Medicaid, in the year following enactment of the funding limitation, there would be an additional 13 babies born that year. These 13 additional babies born out of a total 113 come to be approximately one in nine lives.

Qualitative Impact of the Hyde Amendment

Lest we lose sight of the qualitative reality of two million lives, let us consider this brief story of Claire, a young woman who experienced an unplanned pregnancy at age 17 and said in a recent news article, "I felt hopeless and alone."[8] She explained that if Medicaid funding for an abortion had been available, it would have been tempting to go ahead and have an abortion. Instead, she reached out for support, was accompanied to a pregnancy care center where she saw the first ultrasound of her son, and decided to continue her pregnancy. Now, a year later, Claire reflects: "I don't know what I would do without him… That's my baby."

Of the two million lives saved by the Hyde Amendment, one can only wonder how many of their mothers were in similar situations.

Conclusion

In conclusion, the Hyde Amendment:

- has enjoyed bipartisan support for 40 years,
- was re-affirmed as constitutional in 1980,
- enjoys support from nearly seven in 10 Americans[9] (including even 51 percent of those self-identifying as "pro-choice"; 44 percent of Democrats[10]; 65 percent of African Americans; 61 percent of Latinos; 58 percent of millennials; and 63 percent of women[11]); and
- has saved an estimated two million lives.

For these compelling reasons, the protective language of the Hyde Amendment should not only be retained as enforced policy, but be codified as a permanent law.

---

[8] Dean J. Nowhere to Hyde?, *World Magazine* Vol. 31 No. 19, September 17, 2016, accessed at: https://world.wng.org/2016/09/nowhere_to_hyde

[9] Abortion in America, Knights of Columbus/Marist Poll, 2016, accessed at: http://www.kofc.org/un/en/resources/communications/abortion-america-january2016.pdf "Please tell me if you strongly support, support, oppose, or strongly oppose using tax dollars to pay for a woman's abortion."

[10] http://www.kofc.org/un/en/resources/communications/kofc-arist-poll-banner072016.pdf

[11] http://www.kofc.org/un/en/resources/communications/kofc-arist-poll-bannerb-072016.pdf

Should the Hyde Amendment be repealed in the near future, we now cannot say we were ignorant that – based on comprehensive and current research – approximately 60,000 lives are expected to be lost in the first year alone. Instead, let us continue to support this longstanding bipartisan policy which respects individual conscience of the taxpayer, and has been shown to protect millions of lives.

Thank you again for holding today's hearing on these crucial issues.

———————

Mr. FRANKS. Thank you, Ms. Plaster.

And I would now recognize our third witness, Ms. Johnson.

And, Ms. Johnson, if you would make sure that microphone is turned on.

TESTIMONY OF KIERRA JOHNSON, EXECUTIVE DIRECTOR, UNITE FOR REPRODUCTIVE AND GENDER EQUITY (URGE)

Ms. JOHNSON. Good morning. Thank you for the opportunity to appear before you today to speak about the Hyde amendment, one of our Nation's most harmful and shameful policies, one that singles out low-income women and interferes with their personal decision about whether to end a pregnancy.

My name is Kierra Johnson, and I am the executive director of URGE, Unite for Reproductive and Gender Equity, and as a steering committee member of the All Above All campaign, a campaign led by more than 150 reproductive health, rights, and justice organizations united to lift the bans on abortion coverage.

Safe quality abortion services should be available, regardless of a woman's ability to pay, her source of insurance, or where she lives. However, since the passage of the Hyde amendment in 1976, the appropriations process has been used as a vehicle to systematically deny meaningful access, access to poor women, and has expanded to harm many others.

As a result of the Hyde amendment and its extended reach into similar restrictions, nearly 29 million women of reproductive age do not have insurance coverage of abortion. Each restriction, each ban is intended by anti-abortion politicians to further their ultimate goal of pushing abortion out of reach for as many people as possible.

For those who are struggling to get by, disproportionately women of color, low-income women, young women, immigrant women, a coverage ban might as well be a ban on abortion altogether. Studies have shown that restricting Medicaid coverage of abortion forces one in four low-income women seeking abortion to carry an unwanted pregnancy to term.

The Hyde amendment creates one of the most onerous barriers to abortion care. Just listen to the voices of those who have felt the impact of these bans.

Kendall from Colorado says, "I found out I was pregnant, and I was deceived by the center I visited because it ended up being an anti-choice crisis pregnancy center. After that, I struggled for weeks to find resources, the last $200. I have been anxious, frantic, and terrified. My health has declined, and I believed there was little to no hope until today when I was finally able to access an abortion."

A second woman recounts, "Here is what it took for me to gather the money for my abortion. It was hard. It took 3 weeks. The payday loan I took out for my abortion wiped out my entire account. I got a 3-day notice on my apartment door, and things started to spiral out of control. And then, when I became evicted, I lived in a shelter temporarily."

As a Black woman, I am outraged that the morally bankrupt Hyde amendment has been permitted to persist for so long. It is a source of pain for many women and should be a source of shame for those who support it.

The time for policies that visit indignity and deprivation on women, including Black women is over. Last year, Representatives Barbara Lee, Diana DeGette, and Jan Schakowsky made history by introducing the Equal Access to Abortion Coverage and Health Insurance Act, the EACH Woman Act. This bold legislation respects that each of us, not just some of us, should be able to make our own decisions about pregnancy and prohibits politicians from interfering by withholding coverage for abortion care. With this bill, we are saying that all of us should have access to the same coverage and options, independent of income, ZIP code, or source of insurance.

This legislation now has more than 120 cosponsors in the House and the support of the American people. Polling released last July shows that a majority of Americans would support a bill requiring Medicaid to cover abortion.

A right without access isn't a right at all. In the EACH Woman Act, I see the transformational power of centering the lives, struggles, and aspirations of those for whom the legal right to a safe abortion has not yet been made a reality. But that reality is within our reach. We can work together to build a future where women's decisions are treated with respect and we can get the healthcare we need with dignity and compassion.

Thank you.

[The testimony of Ms. Johnson follows:]

United States House of Representatives Committee on the Judiciary
Subcommittee on the Constitution and Civil Justice

"The Ultimate Civil Right:
Examining the Hyde Amendment
and the Born Alive Infants Protection Act"

Testimony of
Kierra Johnson
Executive Director, URGE: Unite for Reproductive and Gender Equity
Steering Committee Member, All* Above All

September 23, 2016

Mr. Chairman and Distinguished Members of this Subcommittee:

Thank you for the opportunity to appear before you today to speak about the Hyde Amendment,
one of our nation's most harmful and shameful policies; one that singles out low-income women
and interferes with their personal decision about whether to end a pregnancy.

My name is Kierra Johnson, and I'm here as the Executive Director of URGE: Unite for
Reproductive and Gender Equity, an organization that is mobilizing the diverse, upcoming
generation of leaders to promote and protect reproductive rights, sexual health & gender justice,
and also as a steering committee member of All* Above All, a campaign of more than 115
reproductive health, rights and justice organizations united to lift the bans on abortion coverage.

We envision a world in which each of us has the tools we need to pursue our dreams and build
the families and futures we desire. For this to be a reality, a woman must have access to the
full-spectrum of reproductive health care, including abortion.

Safe, quality abortion services should be available regardless of a woman's ability to pay, her
source of insurance, or where she lives. However, since the passage of the Hyde Amendment
in 1976, which bars federal Medicaid funds from covering abortion, the appropriations process
has been used as a vehicle to systematically deny meaningful abortion access to poor women.

THE HYDE AMENDMENT IS A POLITICAL TOOL TO PUSH ABORTION OUT OF REACH
Those who oppose abortion have tried and failed to make it illegal, so instead they have worked
to make it almost impossible to obtain. Thus the Hyde Amendment was the first in a long line of
restrictions after the *Roe v. Wade* Supreme Court decision intended to interfere in women's
health decision around ending a pregnancy.

This isn't speculation. The policy's original author Rep. Henry Hyde stated, "I certainly would like to prevent, if I could legally, anybody having an abortion: a rich woman, a middle-class woman or a poor woman. Unfortunately, the only vehicle available is the... Medicaid bill."

And this policy has a dramatic reach:

- Approximately 1 in 6 women of reproductive age (15-44) are enrolled in Medicaid.[1]
- Sixty percent (60%) of women of reproductive-age enrolled in Medicaid live in states that withhold insurance coverage for abortion except in limited circumstances.[2]
- Fifty-two percent (52%) of women of reproductive-age enrolled in Medicaid and subject to abortion coverage restrictions are women of color.[3]
- Three-fourths of abortion patients were low income as of 2014 with 49% living at less than the federal poverty level, and 26% living at 100–199% of the poverty level.[4]

Not only has Congress passed the Hyde Amendment every year since 1976, but they've also passed additional abortion coverage restrictions that target women based on their source of insurance or care. Hyde-like restrictions have been extended to deny coverage from women enrolled in Medicaid, Medicare and Children's Health Insurance Program; federal employees enrolled in the Federal Employees Health Benefits Plan; Peace Corps volunteers; members of our Armed Forces and their dependents; Native Americans covered by the Indian Health Service; and women being held in federal prisons or detention centers, including those detained for immigration purposes. As a result of the Hyde Amendment and its progeny, nearly 29 million women of reproductive age do not have insurance coverage for abortion.[5]

Most recently, in one of the first acts of the 114th Congress, abortion opponents in the House passed H.R. 7, a sweeping ban on abortion coverage that withholds abortion coverage from virtually all women in the U.S. and takes the unprecedented step of inserting abortion politics into tax policy.

In addition to these federal bans, policymakers in 25 states have restricted coverage of abortion in insurance plans offered through health exchanges and policymakers in 10 of these states have also banned coverage in all private plans.[6] The unprecedented number of abortion restrictions passed across the country – 334 restrictions since 2010[7] – only multiply the hardship of coverage bans.

It is clear that each restriction, each ban, is intended by anti-abortion politicians to further their ultimate goal of pushing abortion out of reach for as many people as possible.

---

[1] Unpublished tabulations using the 2012 and 2013 Current Population Survey (CPS), March Supplements. Via Guttmacher Institute's State Data Center Table Creator. Available at http://www.guttmacher.org/datacenter/table.jsp
[2] Boonstra, H.D., "Abortion in the Lives of Women Struggling Financially: Why Insurance Coverage Matters." Guttmacher Policy Review. Vol. 19 2016. Guttmacher Institute. Jul 2016. Available at https://www.guttmacher.org/about/gpr/2016/07/abortion-lives-women-struggling-financially-why-insurance-coverage-matters
[3] Ibid
[4] Jerman, J., Jones R., and Onda T. "Characteristics of U.S. Abortion Patients in 2014 and Changes Since 2008." Guttmacher Institute. May 2016. Available at https://www.guttmacher.org/sites/default/files/report_pdf/characteristics-us-abortion-patients-2014.pdf
[5] Williamson, H., and Birchler, S. "Infographic: Pass the EACH Woman Act." Center for American Progress. 8 Oct 2015. Available at https://www.americanprogress.org/issues/women/news/2015/10/08/122895/infographic-pass-the-each-woman-act/
[6] "State Policies in Brief: Restricting Insurance Coverage of Abortion (as of June 1, 2016)." Guttmacher Institute. Jun 2016. Available at https://www.guttmacher.org/sites/default/files/state_policy_overview_files/spib_rica.pdf
[7] Nash, E., Gold RB., Ansari-Thomas, Z., Cappello, O., and Mohammed, L. "Laws Affecting Reproductive Health and Rights: State Trends at Midyear, 2016." Guttmacher Institute. 21 Jul 2016. Available at: https://www.guttmacher.org/article/2016/07/laws-affecting-reproductive-health-and-rights-state-trends-midyear-2016

THE HARMFUL IMPACT OF THE HYDE AMENDMENT AND ABORTION COVERAGE BANS

For those who are struggling to make ends meet – disproportionately women of color, low-income women, young people, immigrant women – coverage for abortion can mean the difference between getting the health care they need and being denied that care.

- Studies show that when policymakers place severe restrictions on Medicaid coverage of abortion, it forces one in four poor women seeking an abortion to carry an unwanted pregnancy to term.[8]
- When a woman is living paycheck to paycheck, denying coverage for an abortion could push her deeper into poverty. studies show that a woman who seeks an abortion but is denied is more likely to fall into poverty than one who is able to get an abortion.[9]
- Women with lower socioeconomic status – specifically those who are least able to afford out-of-pocket medical expenses – already experience disproportionately high rates of adverse health conditions. Denying access to abortion care only exacerbates existing health disparities.[10]

Those who do find a way to end their pregnancies often do so at great personal cost. Many are forced to delay their procedure for as long as two to three weeks while they pull together several hundred dollars to pay for the care they need, with the price of the procedure increasing as they raise these funds.[11]

It may not seem like a big expense to a Member of Congress, but finding several hundred dollars in these tough financial times can be difficult. In one study, out-of-pocket costs for an abortion were equivalent to more than one-third of monthly personal income.[12] For many people, abortion care costs more than their monthly rent. Studies show that most Americans do not have enough savings to cover a financial emergency,[13] which means they have to borrow, sell or pawn personal items, or divert money from another financial obligation to cover emergencies such as an unexpected health care need.

Just listen to the voices of those who have felt the impact of these bans. Kendall from Colorado says, "I found out I was pregnant and was deceived by the center I visited because it ended up being an anti-choice crisis pregnancy center. After that I struggled for weeks to find resources and to come up with the last $200. I have been anxious, frantic, and terrified. My health has declined and I believed there was little to no hope until today when I was finally able to access an abortion."

A 27-year-old woman recounted, "Here is what it took to gather the money for my abortion. It was hard, it took me three weeks…. The payday loan [I took out for my abortion] wiped out my entire account…. I got a three-day notice on my apartment door, and things started to spiral out of control and then when I became evicted I lived in a shelter temporarily."

---

[8] Henshaw, S.K., Joyce T., Dennis, A., Finer, L.B., and Blanchard, K. "Restrictions on Medicaid Funding for Abortions: A Literature Review." Guttmacher Institute. Jul 2009. Available at http://www.guttmacher.org/pubs/MedicaidLitReview.pdf

[9] Foster, D.G., Roberts, S.C.M., and Mauldon, J., "Socioeconomic consequences of abortion compared to unwanted birth." abstract presented at the American Public Health Association annual meeting. Oct 2012. Available at https://apha.confex.com/apha/140am/webprogram/Paper263858.html

[10] Ibid

[11] Boonstra, H.D. "Insurance Coverage of Abortion: Beyond the Exceptions for Life Endangerment, Rape and Incest." Guttmacher Policy Review. Vol. 16, No. 3, 2013. Available at http://www.guttmacher.org/pubs/gpr/16/3/gpr160302.html

[12] Roberts S.C., Gould, H., Kimport, K., Weltz, T.A., and Foster, D.G. "Out-of-pocket costs and insurance coverage for abortion in the United States." Women's Health Issues. Mar-Apr 2014. Abstract available at http://www.ncbi.nlm.nih.gov/pubmed/24630423

[13] "Majority of Americans do not have money available to meet an unplanned expense." News Release. National Foundation for Credit Counseling. 5 Aug 2011. Available at https://www.nfcc.org/majority-of-americans-do-not-have-money-available-to-meet-an-unplanned-expense

ENSURING PERSONAL DECISION MAKING FOR EACH OF US

The time for these policies that visit indignity and deprivation on women, including Black women, is over. Last year, Representatives Barbara Lee, Diana DeGette and Jan Schakowsky made history by introducing the Equal Access to Abortion Coverage in Health Insurance Act, known as the EACH Woman Act (H.R. 2972). This bold legislation would reverse the Hyde Amendment and related abortion coverage and care restrictions.

The EACH Woman Act makes a meaningful policy change for women and their families, and creates two important standards for reproductive health:

- First, it sets up the federal government as a standard-bearer, ensuring that every woman who receives care or insurance through the federal government will have coverage for abortion services. The EACH Woman Act restores abortion coverage to those enrolled in a government health insurance plan (i.e., Medicaid, Medicare), including those who live in the District of Columbia; enrolled in a government-managed health insurance program (i.e., FEHBP, TRICARE) due to an employment relationship; or who receive health care from a government provider or program (i.e., Indian Health Services, the Federal Bureau of Prisons, the Veterans Administration).
- Second, it prohibits political interference with decisions by private health insurance companies to offer coverage for abortion care. Federal, state and local legislators will not be able to interfere with the private insurance market, including the insurance marketplaces established by the Affordable Care Act, to prevent insurance companies from providing abortion coverage.

Support for the EACH Woman Act is growing every day. To date, more than 120 members of Congress have united to co-sponsor the EACH Woman Act and 78 national, state and local organizations – including abortion funds, labor unions, groups representing Black, Latina, and Asian American and Pacific Islander (AAPI) communities, and youth organizations – have shown their support for the EACH Woman Act. Further, polling released in July 2015[14] and again this year[15] shows a majority of voters support lifting the Hyde Amendment and ensuring that Medicaid covers all pregnancy-related care, including abortion. Support for lifting the Hyde Amendment is especially strong among Millennials, African Americans, and Hispanics.

In sum, a right without access is no right at all. In the EACH Woman Act, I see the transformational power of centering the lives, struggles, and aspirations of those for whom the legal right to a safe abortion has not yet been made a reality.

But that reality is within our reach. We can work together to build a future where women's decisions are treated with respect and we can get the healthcare we need with dignity and compassion.

---

[14] "Polling on Repealing the Hyde Amendment." Hart Research Associates. Jun 2015. Available at http://allaboveall.org/wp/wp-content/uploads/2016/06/Polling-Memo.pdf
[15] "Battleground Polling on Repealing the Hyde Amendment." Hart Research Associates. Sep 2016 Available at http://allaboveall.org/wp/wp-content/uploads/2016/09/AllAboveAll_Hart_Battleground-Poll-2016-Memo.pdf

A

Mr. FRANKS. Thank you, Ms. Johnson.

And I would now recognize our final witness, Ms. Grossu.

And if you make sure that microphone is on.

TESTIMONY OF ARINA O. GROSSU, M.A., DIRECTOR, CENTER FOR HUMAN DIGNITY, FAMILY RESEARCH COUNCIL

Ms. GROSSU. Chairman Franks, Ranking Member Cohen, and distinguished Members of the Subcommittee, I am grateful and honored to have been invited to testify today in support of the Born-Alive Abortion Survivors Protection Act.

In 2000 and 2001, Jill Stanek testified before this Committee about her experience as a registered nurse where she discovered babies born alive after an attempted abortion and left to die in the department's soiled utility closet.

In 2002, Congress responded by passing the Born-Alive Infants Protection Act, which was signed by President George W. Bush and is current Federal law. It passed by voice vote in the House and with unanimous consent in the Senate.

Unfortunately, incidents involving born-alive children being killed after an attempted abortion have continued after this law and into the present.

Infanticide is unacceptable in a civilized society, regardless of what one may think about abortion itself. Up to 2010, abortionist Kermit Gosnell operated his dirty and dangerous abortion facility where he did hundreds of snippings of born-alive babies as part of his abortion process. The grand jury report noted many of the women ''gave birth before he even got there. When you perform late-term 'abortions' by inducing labor, you get babies. Live, breathing, squirming babies...Gosnell had a simple solution for the unwanted babies he delivered: He killed them...by sticking scissors into the back of the baby's neck and cutting the spinal cord.'' See, for example, the image of Baby Boy B, who was found in his facility.

Federal and State authorities finally raided his facility not because he was illegally killing born-alive infants, but because of his illegal prescription drug activity.

While Gosnell's case was particularly gruesome, he is not an outlier. A former employee of current Texas abortionist Douglas Karpen described how he regularly killed babies born alive by snipping their spinal cords, fatally injuring them with blows to the soft spot on their heads, and twisting their necks.

She said, ''I am pretty sure I was seeing at least three or four large babies that were completely delivered in some way or another daily...When the fetus would come completely out, of course the fetus would still be alive, because it was still moving. Of course you could see the stomach breathing, and that is when he would do this.''

Yet despite the gruesome photo and eyewitness evidence, Karpen was cleared in December 2013.

The Center for Medical Progress, in its investigative videos, authenticated by an in-depth forensic analysis report, revealed a lot of evidence of babies killed after being born alive. For example, Perrin Larton, a procurement manager from Advanced Bioscience Resources, said, ''The whole point is not to have a live birth. I literally have women come in and say they will go into the OR and they are back out in 3 minutes, and I am going, 'What is going on?' Oh, yeah, the fetus was already in the vaginal canal whenever we put her in the stirrups. It just fell out.''

Holly O'Donnell, a former procurement technician with StemExpress, recounted one incident where her supervisor said, ''Want to see something kind of cool?' And she just tapped the heart and it started beating. And I am sitting here, and I am looking at this fetus, and its heart is beating.''

Data that the CDC collects also confirms that babies are born alive after attempted abortions. Between the years 2003 and 2014, there were somewhere between 376 and 588 infant deaths under the medical code P96.4, which keeps track of babies born alive after the termination of pregnancy.

The CDC concluded that of the 588 babies, 143 were definitively born alive after an attempted abortion, and they lived from minutes to 1 or more days, with 48 percent of babies living between 1 to 4 hours.

It also admitted that it is possible the number is an underestimate. We know it is an underestimate because these are just the reported numbers from hospitals, not from the abortion facilities.

Gosnell is only one abortionist who is responsible for hundreds of snippings of born-alive babies, yet he did not report even one. His numbers alone exceed the definitive numbers of the CDC.

Even one baby born alive after an attempted abortion who is then killed is one too many, but we are talking in hundreds of reported ones. Yet not one person, to date, has been charged or convicted under the current Federal law.

Due to developments in technology, babies who are considered extremely pre-term can now survive outside the womb as early as 20 and 21 weeks post-fertilization, recent science journals articles announced, with 67 percent surviving after receiving active care.

Here, for example, is Lucas Moore, who was born at 21 weeks post-fertilization and 1 year later. Dr. David Burchfield, the chief of neonatology at the University of Florida, said, ''It confirms that if you don't do anything, these babies will not make it, and if you do something, some of them will make it.''

This is why we need the proposed Born-Alive Act. It explicitly requires healthcare practitioners to treat born-alive abortion survivors with the same care they would treat any other born-alive baby and admit such babies immediately to the hospital. It provides enforcement mechanisms, such as criminal sanctions and penalties, to hold abortionists accountable for killing born-alive infants. And the bill also expressly excludes any prosecution of the mother of a baby born alive, and it gives her a private right of action to seek relief if the abortionist were to kill her born-alive baby.

The White House has promised that it would veto the born-alive legislation, citing it would have a chilling effect. I cannot think of a more chilling effect than continuing to let U.S. abortionists commit infanticide.

Born-alive babies after attempted abortion are already recognized as legal persons since the 2002 born-alive law. The proposed Born-Alive Abortion Survivors Protection Act simply recognizes the obligations that follow from this reality, to ensure that babies born alive after attempted abortions will be given the best medical care available and full and equal protection under our laws. I earnestly ask that you support this bill to stop infanticide in the United States.

Thank you.

[The testimony of Ms. Grossu follows:]

Arina O. Grossu, M.A.
Director, Center for Human Dignity
Family Research Council

Hearing of the House Judiciary Committee,
Subcommittee on the Constitution and Civil Justice:

On "The Ultimate Civil Right:
Examining the Hyde Amendment and the Born Alive Infants Protection Act."

September 23, 2016
9:00 a.m.
2237 Rayburn Building

Hon. Trent Franks, Chair

Hon. Steve Cohen, Ranking Member

Honorable Members

United States House of Representatives

Committee on the Judiciary

Subcommittee on the Constitution and Civil Justice

2237 Rayburn House Office Building

Washington, DC 20515-6216

Chairman Franks, Ranking Member Cohen, and Distinguished Members of the Subcommittee:

I am grateful to have been invited by the Subcommittee to testify on "The Ultimate Civil Right: Examining the Hyde Amendment and the Born Alive Infants Protection Act." My name is Arina Grossu and I am the Director of the Center for Human Dignity at the Family Research Council (FRC). As a policy analyst, my issues of expertise and research encompass the dignity of human life from conception until natural death.

FRC has long supported the Hyde Amendment, which has prevented government funding for elective abortion for over thirty years and since the 1990's has prevented funding for health plans that include elective abortion coverage. This law, if revoked, would increase the number of abortions in the United States. According to the Guttmacher Institute, "approximately one-fourth of women who would have Medicaid-funded abortions instead give birth when this funding is unavailable."[1] FRC also supports the *Born-Alive Abortion Survivors Protection Act* (H.R. 3504/S. 2066). My remarks will focus on the need for this legislation.

To summarize, I will address the stories which emerged years ago of babies being left to die after attempted abortions. In 2002, Congress responded by passing the *Born-Alive Infants Protection Act*, which was signed by President George W. Bush and is current federal law. This law recognized a child who is born alive after a failed abortion attempt, as a legal person under the

---

[1] Stanley K. Henshaw, et al. "Restrictions on Medicaid Funding for Abortions: A Literature Review," Guttmacher Institute, June 2009, https://www.guttmacher.org/sites/default/files/report_pdf/medicaidlitreview.pdf.

Additional Note: "Studies published over the course of two decades looking at a number of states concluded that 18–35% of women who would have had an abortion continued their pregnancies after Medicaid funding was cut off." In a study examining abortion and birthrates in North Carolina, where the legislature created a special fund to pay for abortions for poor women, researchers found that "one-third of women who would have had an abortion if support were available carried their pregnancies to term when the abortion fund was unavailable." Boonstra, Heather D. "The Heart of the Matter: Public Funding Of Abortion for Poor Women in the United States," Guttmacher Policy Review, Winter 2007, Volume 10, Number 1, p. 16, https://www.guttmacher.org/sites/default/files/article_files/gpr100112.pdf.

laws of the United States. The legal definition of live birth includes any sign of life, such as breath, heartbeat, pulsation of the umbilical cord, or definite movement of voluntary muscles.[2]

Unfortunately, incidents involving born alive children being killed after an attempted abortion have continued after this law was passed. Infanticide is unacceptable in a civilized society, regardless of what one may think about abortion itself. It should be uncontroversial for the federal government to supplement current law with enforcement protections for born-alive children after attempted abortions. That is why Congress must pass the proposed legislation known as the *Born-Alive Abortion Survivors Protection Act* (H.R. 3504/S. 2066).

The Need for the *"Born-Alive Infants Protection Act of 2002"*

In 2000 and 2001, Jill Stanek, a former nurse, testified before this Committee about her experience as a registered nurse in the Labor and Delivery Department at Christ Hospital in Oak Lawn, Illinois, where she discovered babies born alive after an attempted abortion and left to die in the department's soiled utility closet.[3]

Stanek called them "live birth abortions."[4] She recounted, "In this particular abortion procedure doctors do not attempt to kill the baby in the uterus. The goal is simply to prematurely deliver a baby who dies during the birth process or soon afterward." She stated that it is not uncommon for one of these live aborted babies to linger for an hour or two or even longer. One of them once lived for almost eight hours. The babies were not given help to survive.

She described one of those instances: "One night, a nursing co-worker was taking a Down syndrome baby who was aborted alive to our Soiled Utility Room because his parents did not want to hold him, and she did not have time to hold him. I could not bear the thought of this suffering child dying alone in a Soiled Utility Room, so I cradled and rocked him for the 45 minutes that he lived. He was between 21 and 22 weeks old, weighed about 1/2 pound, and was about 10 inches long."

She continued: "Another nurse from Christ Hospital also testified with me in Washington. Allison described walking into the Soiled Utility Room on two separate occasions to find live aborted babies left naked on a scale and the metal counter."

In another testimony she added that a baby was literally thrown into the trash: "A Support Associate told me about a live aborted baby who was left to die on the counter of the Soiled Utility Room wrapped in a disposable towel. This baby was accidentally thrown into the

---

[2] U.S. Congress. House. Judiciary Committee. *Born-Alive Infants Protection Act of 2002*, H.R. 2175, 107 th Cong., 2002, https://www.congress.gov/bill/107th-congress/house-bill/2175/text.

[3] "Testimony of Jill L. Stanek, RN," U.S. House Committee on the Judiciary - Subcommittee on the Constitution and Civil Justice, May 23, 2013, https://judiciary.house.gov/_files/hearings/113th/05232013/Stanek%2005232013.pdf.

[4] Sarah Terzo, "Looking back: Jill Stanek exposed live birth abortions at Illinois hospital." Live Action News, July 25, 2015, accessed September 21, 2016, http://liveactionnews.org/looking-back-jill-stanek-exposed-live-birth-abortions-illinois-hospital/.

garbage, and when they later were going through the trash to find the baby, the baby fell out of the towel and on to the floor."[5]

Stanek also pointed out the ironic juxtaposition between the amount of medical care available to a premature baby who is "wanted" and a live premature baby who is the result of an attempted abortion and deemed "unwanted":

> *"I was recently told about a situation by a nurse who said, 'I can't stop thinking about it.' She had a patient who was 23- weeks pregnant, and it did not look as if her baby would be able to continue to live inside of her. The baby was healthy and had up to a 39% chance of survival, according to national statistics. But the patient chose to abort. The baby was born alive. If the mother had wanted everything done for her baby, there would have been a neonatologist, pediatric resident, neonatal nurse, and respiratory therapist present for the delivery, and the baby would have been taken to our Neonatal Intensive Care Unit for specialized care. Instead, the only personnel present for this delivery were an obstetrical resident and my co-worker. After delivery the baby, who showed early signs of thriving, was merely wrapped in a blanket and kept in the Labor & Delivery Department until she died 2-1/2 hours later."*

To respond to these instances, in 2002, Congress passed and President George W. Bush signed into law the *Born-Alive Infants Protection Act*. In fact, this bill passed by voice vote in the House of Representatives and with unanimous consent in the Senate. The law reasonably stated that the terms "person," "human being," "child," and "individual" shall include "every infant member of the species homo sapiens who is born alive at any stage of development."[6]

Instances of Babies Born Alive After an Attempted Abortion in the U.S.
Since the Enactment of the 2002 Federal Born-Alive Law

The numerous instances of babies who continue to be born alive and killed in the United States despite the 2002 *Born Alive Infants Protection Act* federal law demonstrates the urgent need for the enforcement provisions in the *Born-Alive Abortion Survivors Protection Act* (H.R. 3504/S. 2066).

Abortionist Kermit Gosnell operated his dirty and dangerous Philadelphia abortion business and committed horrendous crimes in Philadelphia for over three decades. His facility went nearly two decades without being inspected by Pennsylvania health officials, despite numerous complaints that were filed against him with the Pennsylvania Department of Health, Pennsylvania Department of State, and the Philadelphia Department of Public Health. The Pennsylvania Department of Health conducted inadequate and sporadic inspections for thirteen years and then no inspections at all for seventeen years between 1993 and 2010. The Grand Jury report detailed that the Pennsylvania Department of Health's policy of not inspecting Gosnell's

---

[5] "Testimony from Nurse Jill L. Stanek during the Born Alive Infant Protection Act Congressional Hearings," California ProLife Council, accessed September 21, 2016, http://www.californiaprolife.org/testimony-from-nurse-jill-l-stanek-during-the-born-alive-infant-protection-act-congressional-hearings/.
[6] *Born-Alive Infants Protection Act of 2002*, https://www.congress.gov/bill/107th-congress/house-bill/2175/text.

facility during Governor Ridge's administration "was motivated by a desire not to be 'putting a barrier up to women' seeking abortions."[7]

Until 2010, Gosnell got away with physically injuring many of his patients, causing the death of at least one woman, Karnamaya Mongar, and killing countless babies in-utero as well as babies born alive. Not even Mongar's death triggered an inspection or investigation.

His heinous and murderous practices of snipping the spines of born-alive children were only discovered by accident when federal and state authorities raided his facility in 2010, not because he was illegally killing born-alive infants, but because of his illegal prescription drug activity. The current federal law was not the impetus for first investigating Gosnell, who clearly had been snipping the spines of born-alive children for many years.

Gosnell often snipped the necks of babies born alive as part of his abortion process. The Grand Jury Report described Gosnell's process:

> *"Babies that big are hard to get out. Gosnell's approach, whenever possible, was to force full labor and delivery of premature infants on ill-informed women... Many of them gave birth before he even got there. When you perform late-term 'abortions' by inducing labor, you get babies. Live, breathing, squirming babies. By 24 weeks, most babies born prematurely will survive if they receive appropriate medical care. But that was not what the Women's Medical Society was about. Gosnell had a simple solution for the unwanted babies he delivered: he killed them. He didn't call it that. He called it 'ensuring fetal demise.' The way he ensured fetal demise was by sticking scissors into the back of the baby's neck and cutting the spinal cord."*

Although the Grand Jury Report detailed that there were "hundreds of snippings," most of them could not be prosecuted because Gosnell destroyed the files. As a result, Gosnell was convicted of first degree murder in 2013 in the deaths of only three of the infants born alive after an attempted abortion and involuntary manslaughter in the death of Karnamaya Mongar.

While Gosnell's case was particularly gruesome, he is not an outlier.[8] For example, three former employees of current Texas abortionist Douglas Karpen[9] came forward to reveal the infanticide and stomach-turning practices that went on in Karpen's facility. Deborah Edge, one of those former employees, described how Karpen regularly killed babies born alive by snipping their spinal cords, fatally injuring them with blows to the soft spot on their heads, and twisting their necks. Ms. Edge described:

> *When he did an abortion, especially in an over twenty week abortion, most of the time the fetus would come completely out before he either cut the spinal cord or introduced one of*

[7] "Report of the Grand Jury," Court of Common Pleas – First Judicial District of Pennsylvania – Criminal Trial Division, January 14, 2011, p. 147, http://www.phila.gov/districtattorney/pdfs/grandjurywomensmedical.pdf.
[8] "Worst Offenders," AbortionDocs.org, accessed September 21, 2016, http://abortiondocs.org/worst-offenders/.
[9] Sarah Terzo, "Abortion clinic workers share how babies are born alive and killed." Live Action News, August 19, 2015, accessed September 21, 2016, http://liveactionnews.org/abortion-clinic-workers-share-how-babies-are-born-alive-killed/.

the instruments into the soft spot [of the head] of the fetus in order to kill the fetus...I think every morning I saw several, on several occasions, if we had, maybe twenty patients of course, maybe ten or twelve or fifteen patients would be large procedures, and out of those large procedures, I'm pretty sure I was seeing at least three or four that were completely delivered in some way or another.

And most of the time we would see him, when the fetus would come completely out, of course the fetus would still be alive, because it was still moving... of course you could see the stomach breathing and that's when he would do his – he would snap the spine as they're saying that this doctor [Kermit Gosnell] did and of course the soft spot was where he would take one of the forceps... the dilators, and he would stick it into the soft spot of the fetus's head.

Yet, despite the gruesome photo and eyewitness evidence,[10] Karpen was cleared in December 2013 by the same Harris County District Attorney, Devon Anderson, who indicted David Daleiden in January 2016, although all charges against Daleiden were dismissed by July 2016.

Additional reports indicate killing born-alive babies may be more routine than these instances suggest. Videos and transcripts released in the summer of 2015 by the Center for Medical Progress (CMP) revealed this is a much more common practice than the abortion industry would have the public believe.[11] It is important to note that CMP investigative videos have been confirmed as completely authentic in an in-depth forensic analysis by Coalfire Systems Inc., a highly accredited and independent forensic analysis and cybersecurity company that does work for Fortune 500 companies.[12]

The videos show top Planned Parenthood directors and abortionists discussing the harvesting of baby body parts. Their discussions of "intact" babies should be of particular interest to this Subcommittee.

"Intact" babies are usually born alive, unless they are first poisoned with digoxin, a chemical drug used in later-term abortions to cause the death of the baby to prevent a live birth from occurring. An "intact" delivery, whether for an abortion or not, usually signifies a baby is born alive. If the baby was not born alive in an "intact" delivery, most physicians would add some other qualifier such as "miscarriage" or "stillborn."

---

[10] "Special Report: New Stunning Photos, Testimony Show Texas Abortionist Kills Babies Born Alive," Operation Rescue, May 15, 2013, accessed September 21, 2016, http://www.operationrescue.org/archives/special-report-new-stunning-photos-testimony-show-texas-abortionist-kills-babies-born-alive/.
[11] "Investigative Footage," The Center for Medical Progress, accessed September 21, 2016, http://www.centerformedicalprogress.org/cmp/investigative-footage/.
[12] The report concluded: "Coalfire's analysis of the recorded media files contained on the flash drive indicates that the video recordings are authentic and show no evidence of manipulation or editing. This conclusion is supported by the consistency of the video file date and time stamps, the video timecode, as well as the folder and file naming scheme. The uniformity between the footage from the cameras from the two Investigators also support the evidence that the video recordings are authentic." Source: "Digital Forensics Analysis Report," Alliance Defending Freedom, November 5, 2015, accessed September 22, 2016, http://www.adfmedia.org/files/CoalfireCMPvideosReport.pdf.

CMP's videos revealed that the abortionists and directors involved did not prefer to poison the baby with digoxin because the procurement companies would not accept baby body parts that had been "tainted" with the chemical, causing the baby's stem cells to be unusable for research purposes.

An intact and digoxin-free delivery during an abortion essentially means a live birth.

First, Deborah Nucatola, Planned Parenthood Federation of America's Senior Director of Medical Services, described an abortion procedure that sounded very similar to the illegal partial-birth abortion which involved switching the baby to breech position to get the baby's body parts intact. Speaking about how abortionists get around the "Federal [Partial-Birth] Abortion Ban" to extract intact fetuses prime for organ harvesting, Nucatola noted a split among abortionists. Some "providers who use digoxin use" it to "induce [fetal] demise" prior to the procedure to avoid falling under the ban, which only applies to a "live" baby. Others, she noted, who do partial-birth abortions without using digoxin to "induce demise" prior, say that "partial-birth abortion" is "not a medical term, it doesn't exist in reality," and "so there are some people who interpret it [the federal partial birth abortion ban] as intent. So if I say on Day 1 I do not intend to do this, what ultimately happens doesn't matter. Because I didn't intend to do this on Day 1 so I'm complying with the law." Nucatola advised: "If you want no dig[oxin], your options are UCSF and Planned Parenthood New York City."[13]

Second, Jennefer Russo, Medical Director at Planned Parenthood of Orange & San Bernardino Counties in California, also mentioned changing the baby's position and said that having "fully intact specimens...happens sometimes, but it's pretty rare" and they "try" not to have it. While she claimed that they try not to have what is essentially a live birth, she still admitted that it happens sometimes. Russo also confirmed that they do not use the poison digoxin, which means that any intact babies are born alive: "There's a nationwide shortage of dig[oxin]... We don't 'Dig' right now."[14] CMP investigators called one of procurement companies that Russo said the Planned Parenthood affiliate worked with, Da Vinci Biosciences, LLC, and a sales representative confirmed their fetal specimens do not have digoxin saying, "My assumption would be that it is feticide-free, considering that we have such a large catalogue of fetal tissue that I believe that would be a requirement for us, in order to have so many fetal products available."[15] A procurement company could not have "such a large catalogue" of baby body parts unless the baby body parts were free of digoxin.

Third, Melissa Farrell, Director of Research of Planned Parenthood Gulf Coast, advertised the Texas Planned Parenthood branch's track record of its ability to deliver fully intact babies and that they were "just a matter of line items."[16]

[13] "FULL FOOTAGE: Planned Parenthood Uses Partial-Birth Abortions to Sell Baby Parts," YouTube, July 14, 2015, accessed September 22, 2016, https://www.youtube.com/watch?v=H4UjlM9B9KQ.
[14] "FULL FOOTAGE: Planned Parenthood Orange County Changes Abortions to Harvest Intact Fetuses," YouTube, March 1, 2016, accessed September 22, 2016, https://www.youtube.com/watch?v=U9zz_d5BYTM.
[15] Ibid.
[16] "FULL FOOTAGE: Intact Fetuses "Just a Matter of Line Items" for Planned Parenthood TX Mega-Center," YouTube, August 6, 2015, accessed September 22, 2016, https://www.youtube.com/watch?v=MCiD9_ICt44.

Fourth, Savita Ginde, Vice President and Medical Director of the Planned Parenthood of the Rocky Mountains admitted, "Sometimes, we get- if someone delivers before we get to see them for a procedure, then they are intact, but that's not what we go for."[17] Delivering before an abortion procedure means there is a born-alive baby. She admitted that "less than ten percent" of their second trimester babies are born "intact" before the abortion procedure is finished. Even *one* baby born alive after an attempted abortion who is then killed, is one too much.

Fifth, Perrin Larton, a procurement manager from Advanced Bioscience Resources, even admitted that sometimes babies are born alive: "The whole point is not to have a live birth'' but when women who have had "six pregnancies and six vaginal deliveries" come in for an abortion, they have quick deliveries. Larton wondered, "I literally have had women come in and they'll go in the O.R. and they're back out in three minutes, and I'm going, 'What's going on?' Oh yeah, the fetus was already in the vaginal canal whenever we put her in the stirrups. It just fell out."[18]

Sixth, another video showed StemExpress' CEO Cate Dyer, who may soon be held in contempt of Congress along with Stem Express for refusing to comply with a subpoena by the House Select Investigative Panel on Infant Lives, admitted that they get "intact" babies from the abortion facilities they work with shipped to their laboratory. "Case" is the clinical term for an individual baby in the context of this dialogue. Dyer said: "I mean if you had intact cases, which we've done a lot, we sometimes ship those back to our lab in its entirety."[19]

Seventh, in another video, Holly O'Donnell, a former procurement technician with StemExpress, described her harvesting of intact babies post-abortion at Planned Parenthood Mar Monte's Alameda facility in San Jose, which does abortions up to 20 weeks of pregnancy. O'Donnell recounted one incident where her supervisor said, 'I want to see something kind of cool...And she just taps the heart, and it starts beating. And I'm sitting here and I'm looking at this fetus, and its heart is beating, and I don't know what to think." O'Donnell remarked, "I don't know if that constitutes it's technically dead, or it's alive... She gave me the scissors and told me that I had to cut down the middle of the face. I can't even describe what that feels like." O'Donnell also recounted an incident in which she "saw a message saying that the doctor had aborted a fully intact fetus, fully intact, and StemExpress was sending it straight to the lab."[20]

In another part of this video, Ben Van Handel, the Executive Director of Novogenix Laboratories, LLC, which works with Planned Parenthood in San Diego and other abortion facilities nationwide admitted that during procedures to extract the hearts from intact babies from

---

[17] "FULL FOOTAGE: Planned Parenthood VP Says Fetuses May Come Out Intact, Agrees Payments...." YouTube, July 30, 2015, accessed September 22. 2016, https://www.youtube.com/watch?v=wV2U9unI1NM.
[18] "FULL FOOTAGE: Planned Parenthood Pacific Southwest Dr. Katharine Sheehan," YouTube, September 1, 2015, accessed September 22, 2016, https://www.youtube.com/watch?v=69mC-B9aFJk and "FULL FOOTAGE: Planned Parenthood Baby Parts Vendor Advanced Bioscience Resources." YouTube, September 1, 2015, accessed September 22, 2016, https://www.youtube.com/watch?v=fWJb78ynVT8.
[19] "FULL FOOTAGE: Planned Parenthood Baby Parts Buyer StemExpress Wants "Another 50 Livers/Week"," YouTube, August 27, 2015, accessed September 22, 2016, https://www.youtube.com/watch?v=jCQno6hdU6s.
[20] "Human Capital - Episode 3: Planned Parenthood's Custom Abortions for Superior Product." Youtube, August 19, 2015, accessed September 22, 2015, https://youtu.be/FzMAycMMXp8

abortions, "there are times when after the procedure is done that the heart actually is still beating."[21]

One has to wonder how many of those "fully intact" babies were first born alive. If an enforcement mechanism had been in place to protect those babies and prosecute abortionists and staff who violated federal law, perhaps some of these babies would still be alive today. These are just some of the stories that have emerged. There are many others which we do not know about because of lack of reporting, cover-ups by the abortion industry, and witnesses being afraid to share their testimonies.

U.S. Statistics on Babies Born Alive After Termination of Pregnancy

While anecdotal stories offer a window into the practice of the killing of babies born alive after an attempted abortion, even the federal government admits it happens and statistical evidence validates that it happens even more than we may think. Data reports from the Centers for Disease Control and Prevention (CDC) show the incidence of born-alive abortion survivors who are killed in the United States.

The CDC collects mortality records statistics including on the underlying cause of death of infants.[22] Infants born alive after "termination of pregnancy, affecting fetus and newborn" are classified under the ICD-10 code P96.4.[23] Those who are classified under this code are infants who are born alive after a miscarriage as well as those born alive after an attempted abortion.

Two CDC databases show that between the years 2003 and 2014 there were somewhere between 376[24] and 588[25] infant deaths of babies born alive under the ICD-10 code P96.4.[26]

In one review, the CDC determined by looking at the cause-of-death of the 588 babies, that 143 of the infant deaths could "definitively" be classified as infants born alive after an attempted

---

[21] Ibid.

[22] The National Vital Statistics System (NVSS) Mortality Data is provided through contracts between the National Center for Health Statistics (NCHS) and "vital registration systems operated in the various jurisdictions legally responsible for the registration of vital events – births, deaths, marriages, divorces, and fetal deaths."
"National Vital Statistics System," Centers for Disease Control and Prevention, accessed September 21, 2016, http://www.cdc.gov/nchs/nvss/.

[23] The International Classification of Diseases (ICD) 10th revision created by the World Health Organization lists ICD-10 code P96.4 as "Termination of pregnancy, affecting fetus and newborn." "Termination of pregnancy, affecting fetus and newborn," ICD-CODE.org, accessed September 21, 2016, http://www.icd-code.org/codes/p96-4-termination-of-pregnancy-affecting-fetus-and-newborn.

[24] Centers for Disease Control and Prevention, National Center for Health Statistics. Underlying Cause of Death 1999-2014 on CDC WONDER Online Database, released 2015. Data are from the Multiple Cause of Death Files, 1999-2014, as compiled from data provided by the 57 vital statistics jurisdictions through the Vital Statistics Cooperative Program. Accessed at http://wonder.cdc.gov/ucd-icd10.html on September 21, 2016.

[25] "Mortality Records with Mention of International Classification of Diseases-10 code P96.4 (Termination of Pregnancy): United States, 2003-2014," Centers for Disease Control and Prevention, accessed September 21, 2016, http://www.cdc.gov/nchs/health_policy/mortality-records-mentioning-termination-of-pregnancy.htm

[26] The discrepancy in the numbers of the two databases shows a need for more standardized system for reporting babies born alive under the ICD-10 code P96.4 and it also shows a need to notate more clearly whether or not they were spontaneous terminations of pregnancy (miscarriage), induced terminations of pregnancy (abortion), the degree of care administered (if any), and the cause of their death.

abortion. However, it admits that "it is possible that this number (143) underestimates the total number of deaths involving induced termination [abortion]."[27]

Those 143 babies "definitively" born alive after an attempted abortion lived *from minutes to one or more days*, with 47.6% of the babies living between one to four hours. What kind of care, if any, were they given?

It is crucial to note that these are just the *reported* numbers of babies born alive after attempted abortions and may not reflect actual numbers. They do not reflect the facilities that did not choose to report information about babies born alive at their center after an attempted abortion. Gosnell is only one abortionist who was responsible for "hundreds of snippings" of born-alive babies, yet he did not report them to the CDC. His numbers *alone* exceed the "definitive" numbers of the CDC collected data. It was not in his interest to report them. How many other abortionists and facilities currently fail to report babies born alive in their facilities and get away with infanticide without any criminal penalties?

The 2002 federal born-alive law does not have any reporting requirements or any enforcement protections. The anecdotal information and CDC data show the urgent need for Congress to pass the *Born-Alive Abortion Survivors Protection Act* (H.R. 3504/S. 2066) to stop the brutal killing of America's youngest and most vulnerable persons, who have a right to full legal protection under our current laws.

The proposed *Born-Alive* bill would require mandatory reporting of violations if an abortionist or staff member fails to provide care for a baby born alive after an attempted abortion. Killing babies born alive after an attempted abortion is infanticide and it must be enforced as such in our federal laws.

Can Babies Born Alive After an Attempted Abortion Survive?

There are about 5,000 premature babies born annually in the U.S. between 20 to 21 weeks post-fertilization.[28] [29]

Due to developments in technology, babies who are considered "extremely preterm" can now survive outside the womb as early as 20 weeks post-fertilization, if medically treated, a May 2015 *New England Journal of Medicine* study revealed. The study looked at nearly 5,000 extremely premature babies born between 22 and 27 weeks gestation. Of babies who were

---

[27] "Mortality Records with Mention of International Classification of Diseases-10 code P96.4 (Termination of Pregnancy): United States, 2003-2014".

[28] Pam Belluck, "Premature Babies May Survive at 22 Weeks if Treated, Study Finds," *The New York Times*, May 6, 2015, accessed September 22, 2016, http://www.nytimes.com/2015/05/07/health/premature-babies-22-weeks-viability-study.html?_r=0.

[29] Fetal age can be given as age "post-fertilization" meaning the time from conception, or gestational age meaning the time since the last menstrual period (LMP), which is usually easier to determine and occurs approximately two weeks before ovulation and fertilization. Thus gestational age will be 2 weeks older than post-fertilization age, i.e., 22 weeks gestation is equal to 20 weeks post-fertilization.

actively treated at 20 weeks post-fertilization, 23% survived. Of babies actively treated at 21 weeks post-fertilization, 33% survived.[30]

Another July 2016 study about the survival among infants at 20 to 21 weeks post-fertilization following active prenatal and postnatal care showed that 67% of the infants who received active care survived until hospital discharge without severe complications.[31]

The 2002 federal born alive law requires that all babies born alive "at any stage of development" after an attempted abortion be protected. The supplemental *Born-Alive* legislation would make sure that this is enforced.

Under the proposed legislation, care must be given to any infant born alive regardless of gestational age. Immediate care becomes even more critical for infants who can feel pain (between 18-20 weeks post-fertilization)[32] and who can survive if given active treatment (as early as 20 weeks post-fertilization).

Dr. David Burchfield, the chief of neonatology at the University of Florida, said about the May 2015 study, "It confirms that if you don't do anything, these babies will not make it, and if you do something, some of them will make it."[33]

The *Born-Alive Abortion Survivors Protection Act* (H.R. 3504/ S. 2066)

No person to date has been charged or convicted under the *Born-Alive Infants Protection Act of 2002*. Even Kermit Gosnell was only convicted of murder under Pennsylvania state law for

---

[30] Matthew A. Rysavy, Lei Li, et al., "Between-Hospital Variation in Treatment and Outcomes in Extremely Preterm Infants," *The New England Journal of Medicine* 372 (2015), http://www.nejm.org/doi/pdf/10.1056/NEJMoa1410689. Note: Of the 357 babies born at 22 weeks gestation (20 weeks post-fertilization), 79 were actively treated. Eighteen of the 79 babies who were actively treated survived (23%). Of the 755 babies born at 23 weeks gestation (21 weeks post-fertilization), 542 were actively treated. Of the 542 who were actively treated, 180 babies survived (33%).

[31] Katrin Mehler, André Oberthuer, et al., "Survival Among Infants Born at 22 or 23 Weeks' Gestation Following Active Prenatal and Postnatal Care," *JAMA Pediatrics* 170 (2016). More specifically, "of 106 liveborn infants (45 born at 22 weeks and 61 born at 23 weeks and 6 days), 20 (19%) received palliative care (17 born at 22 weeks and 3 born at 23 weeks), and 86 (81%) received active care (28 born at 22 weeks and 58 born at 23 weeks). Of the 86 infants who received active care (mean [SD] maternal age, 32 [6] years), 58 (67%) survived until hospital discharge (17 born at 22 weeks and 41 born at 23 weeks). Eighty-five infants survived without severe complications, with 1 infant born at 22 weeks excluded because of missing data."

[32] Dr. Jean A. Wright, who testified before this Subcommittee in 2005 stated: *After 20 weeks of gestation [18 weeks post-fertilization], an unborn child has all the prerequisite anatomy, physiology, hormones, neurotransmitters, and electrical current to "close the loop" and create the conditions needed to perceive pain... The development of the perception of pain begins at the sixth week of life. By 20 weeks [18 weeks post-fertilization], and perhaps even earlier, all the essential components of anatomy, physiology, and neurobiology exist to transmit painful sensations from the skin to the spinal cord and to the brain.* Source: U.S. Congress. House. Judiciary Committee. *Pain of the Unborn*, 109th Cong., 1s sess., November 1, 2005, http://commdocs.house.gov/committees/judiciary/hju24284.000/hju24284_0.htm.
For more information about What Science Reveals About Fetal Pain, see: http://downloads.frc.org/EF/EF15A104.pdf.

[33] Pam Belluck, *The New York Times*.

snipping the necks of babies. The only federal crime that Gosnell was convicted of were charges of conspiracy to distribute controlled substances to which he pled guilty.

The proposed *Born-Alive* legislation explicitly states that killing born-alive babies is murder under federal law. It would protect babies born alive, no matter in which state they are born.

In response to this continued problem of the born-alive deaths due to the lack of enforcement in current federal law, Congress must pass the *Born-Alive Abortion Survivors Protection Act* (H.R. 3504/S. 2066) sponsored by Rep. Trent Franks (R-AZ) in the House and Sen. Ben Sasse (R-NE) in the Senate. The House passed this bill by a vote of 248-177 in 2015, but the Senate has not yet taken action.

The *Born-Alive Abortion Survivors Protection Act* (H.R. 3504/S. 2066) is a modest bill. First, it provides enforcement mechanisms to current federal law to hold abortionists accountable for killing born-alive infants after an attempted abortion. Second, it explicitly requires health care practitioners to treat born-alive abortion survivors with the same care they would treat any other baby born at the same gestational age, and admit such babies immediately to a hospital. Third, the bill includes criminal sanctions against anyone who intentionally kills an infant born alive. Fourth, it requires any violations to be reported to state or federal law agencies, and creates penalties for failure to report such violations. Fifth, the bill also expressly excludes any prosecution of the mother of a child born alive, and it gives her a private right of action to seek relief if an abortionist were to kill her born-alive infant. A mother should, of course, have a right to sue a doctor who kills her born-alive child, whether directly or through intentional neglect.

As noted, a key provision in the bill requires abortionists and other practitioners to treat a child born alive after an attempted abortion with "the same degree of professional skill, care, and diligence to preserve the life and health of the child as a reasonably diligent and conscientious health care practitioner would render to any other child born alive at the same gestational age" and second, "would ensure that the child born alive is immediately transported and admitted to a hospital."[34]

Some of these provisions may, in effect, require that abortion facilities have basic medical supplies and procedures in place to quickly respond to a live birth after an attempted abortion. In addition to adequately trained and prepared staff, some of the items that an abortion facility should have include an oxygen mask that would fit a newborn, a tracheal tube to intubate a newborn, blankets, and warming pads. The facility should also have protocol in place to immediately transport the baby to the hospital.[35]

---

[34] U.S. Congress. House. Judiciary Committee. *Born-Alive Abortion Survivors Protection Act*, H.R. 3504, 114th Cong., 1s sess., 2015, Sec. 3, 1532, https://www.congress.gov/bill/114th-congress/house-bill/3504/text

[35] In May 2016, the Select Investigative Panel on Infant Lives subpoenaed notorious late-term Maryland abortionist LeRoy Carhart and is seeking information into the policy and procedures at his facility for infants born alive after an attempted abortion. Some of the documents that he is required to present include "any training provided to staff on how to care for an infant born alive"... "the presence of any equipment that serves infants born alive or persons trained to provide neonatal care for an infant born alive"... "the dates on which any child was born alive at LC entities, the person(s) who assisted with the care of that child, and the disposition of the child, including any death certificates prepared for that child and any related referrals to a funeral home." Subpoena available here:

As the proposed legislation states, "Any infant born alive after an abortion or within a hospital, clinic, or other facility has the same claim to the protection of the law that would arise for any newborn, or for any person who comes to a hospital, clinic, or other facility for screening and treatment or otherwise becomes a patient within its care."[36]

Despite the importance of this bill, the White House issued a "Statement of Administration Policy," shocking in its callousness, which promises that the President would veto the *Born-Alive* legislation because the bill would have a "chilling" effect on "the provision of abortion services."[37] This could not be farther from the truth. I cannot think of a more chilling effect than continuing to let abortionists get away with infanticide, the intentional killing of born-alive, breathing babies after an attempted abortion.

Conclusion

Born-alive babies after an attempted abortion are already recognized as legal persons under the laws of the United States since the 2002 enactment of the *Born-Alive Infants Protection Act*. The *Born-Alive Abortion Survivors Protection Act* (H.R. 3504/S. 2066) simply recognizes the obligations that follow from this reality, to ensure that babies born alive after attempted abortions will be given the best medical care available and the full and equal protection of our laws. I earnestly ask that you support this bill to stop infanticide in the United States.

---

https://energycommerce.house.gov/sites/republicans.energycommerce.house.gov/files/documents/114/letters/201605 11CarhartPersonalLetter.pdf

[36] *Born-Alive Abortion Survivors Protection Act*. Sec 2.2.

[37] "Statement of Administration Policy," Executive Office of the President, September 16, 2015, https://www.whitehouse.gov/sites/default/files/omb/legislative/sap/114/saphr3134-3504r_20150916.pdf.

Mr. FRANKS. Thank you, Ms. Grossu.

Mr. JORDAN. Mr. Chairman.

Mr. FRANKS. Does the gentleman have a question?

Mr. JORDAN. Would you yield for just a second. Mr. Chairman, I have got to run to a different Committee. I just wanted to thank our witnesses.

Mr. FRANKS. Could I yield to the gentleman first? I think that there was a video that the gentleman was going to allow. Could I yield to the—I will yield to the gentleman first for questions. We will not begin our question time, and I will yield to the gentleman first.

Mr. JORDAN. I don't have a question. I just have to be at another hearing.

Mr. FRANKS. Then would you yield for the video?

Mr. JORDAN. I will yield for the video, sure.

Mr. FRANKS. All right. If you will start the video there. Thank you, Mr. Jordan.

What we will do, I will go ahead—what we are going to do is we are going to go ahead and suspend for the moment, and I will recognize Mr. DeSantis for 5 minutes.

And thank you, Mr. Jordan.

Mr. JORDAN. Mr. Chair, I have got to run out of here. I want to just thank all our witnesses, in particular Ms. Jessen for her powerful and compelling story. I have got to run to another hearing.

Mr. FRANKS. Thank you, sir, for being here.

Mr. DeSANTIS. Thank you, Mr. Chairman.

The Born-Alive Infants Protection Act of 2002 clarifies that infants who are born alive during abortions or attempted abortions are afforded all legal protections enjoyed by other persons in the United States.

Would you support amendments to that Federal Born-Alive Infants Protection Act to protect infants born into these incredibly vulnerable circumstances by providing a requirement that abortion providers or their staff immediately call 911 for an emergency transfer to a hospital of an infant born alive at a clinic in those circumstances?

Ms. JOHNSON. I am not a medical professional, and what I do know is that there are leading medical organizations that have come out in opposition to this bill. I know that there has been testimony that has been provided for the record, and I think, for me, yielding to their expertise is where I would go.

Mr. DeSANTIS. But why would you—I mean, to me, it is not a question of—I mean, if you have an infant that is born alive, I mean, we have obviously had very powerful testimony, what would you lose by providing the infant treatment at that point?

Ms. JOHNSON. We currently have laws that hold doctors to high standards of care in this country. So, for me, I don't understand why we would necessarily need an additional law around this. But again, I am here as a witness around the Hyde amendment, and like I said, I think there is testimony around this.

Mr. DeSANTIS. Well, let's talk about the Hyde amendment. Would you agree that from a policymaker's perspective, if there is something that you don't like and you tax it, you are likely to get less of it, correct?

Ms. JOHNSON. I am sorry. Can you restate that?

Mr. DESANTIS. If there is something that you don't like as a policymaker, cigarettes, let's say, and you tax it, you will get less people to buy cigarettes, correct?

Ms. JOHNSON. Not necessarily

Mr. DESANTIS. Okay. So if you tax something, you get less of it. You disagree with that. I have think most economists would say that is connect.

If you subsidize something, you then get more of it. Do you agree with that or no?

Ms. JOHNSON. What I agree with is that women choose abortion services, and abortion——

Mr. DESANTIS. That is not what I asked, though. I asked that by providing taxpayer subsidies for something, you are likely to get more of that, correct?

Ms. JOHNSON. I am not sure—I mean, are we talking about public insurance?

Mr. DESANTIS. I am talking about generally. So, for example, I think your testimony, after listening to it, it seems to be that you are upset that there is not public money being provided for abortions, and to me, the takeaway from that is the policy outcome that you are seeking is to increase the number of abortions that are done in the United States. Is that accurate?

Ms. JOHNSON. No.

Mr. DESANTIS. Why would you not get more if you are subsidizing the conduct?

Ms. JOHNSON. Women choose abortion as a part of their health care.

Mr. DESANTIS. But that has nothing to do—but that is a different question from whether the taxpayer should subsidize it. Yes, people have the ability to choose one way or another. People have the ability to choose to do other things in other aspects of life. The question is, is by putting the weight of the taxpayer behind something, you will inevitably lead to increases in abortions, will you not?

Ms. JOHNSON. Well, the American public is in support of Medicaid covering a full range of pregnancy options.

Mr. DESANTIS. That wasn't the—that is not the question. I didn't ask what the American public is for. I am saying, what you are arguing, I just want to tease out the implication, is that you are effectively arguing that we need to increase the amount of abortions that are conducted in the United States.

Ms. JOHNSON. We need to increase the ability for women to make the decisions that they want to make.

Mr. DESANTIS. Well, the ability is there. The question is, how you are going to apply the taxpayer's use of tax dollars? And I think that by not answering the question, I think you have answered it, which is effectively, under your testimony, you would see more abortions in the United States.

And it is a difference between whether you can get one or not. I think most people, even people on either side of the pro-life issue, there has been a general consensus in society we would like to reduce the number of abortions in any way that we can.

So one final question just, Ms. Grossu, before my time has expired.

Ms. Johnson, she said she wasn't here to talk about the born alive, but she said, why would that be necessary? So I am going to ask you, why would we need to do amendments to the Born-Alive Act?

Ms. GROSSU. Thank you, Congressman.

Essentially, there have been no prosecutions under current Federal law. So the Born-Alive Act, which passed in 2002, not one abortionist, not one facility has been convicted under this, although the CDC reports that there are at least 143 born-alive infants after attempted abortions. So what happened to those infants? Were they given care?

And so the question is, this bill, what this bill does is it requires and it creates an enforcement mechanism so that if an abortionist does not provide immediate care to a born-alive infant, that that abortionist is going to have to face violations and fines and criminal penalties for this, and it protects the mother, too, from any kind of criminal penalties.

Mr. DESANTIS. Thank you. My time has expired. I yield back

Mr. FRANKS. I thank the gentleman, and I now recognize the Ranking Member for 5 minutes.

Mr. COHEN. Thank you, Mr. Chairman.

First, I would like to introduce for the record letters from 18 health provider organizations, different religions, different medical specialties, et cetera, into the record.

Mr. FRANKS. Without objection.*

Mr. COHEN. And then I would like to yield my time to the only woman who is here on the panel that can most appropriately ask questions on behalf of the majority——

Mr. FRANKS. All four of our panelists are women, of course.

Mr. COHEN. I apologize, on the congressional panel, and who represents the majority population sexually in this country, Ms. Chu.

Ms. CHU. Thank you, Congressman Cohen. I appreciate the time. And please excuse me. I will have to leave right after this because I have to catch my flight back to Los Angeles.

I want to thank Kierra Johnson for testifying today and for bringing to light the negative impact that the Hyde amendment has on women all across the United States. For 40 years, the Hyde amendment has been used to deny a woman coverage for abortion just because she is poor; and because of social and economic inequality, women of color are even more disproportionately impacted.

A low-income woman is able to use Medicaid for her healthcare needs, except in one area, abortion, due to the Hyde amendment. Because of the lack of funds, she is crippled from making one of most critical health decision she could ever make, a personal decision best made by her and her doctor and not politicians.

In order to pay for the abortion, she may forego paying utility bills, rent, or food, or sell personal belongs, but then, due to the

---

*Note: The submitted material is not printed in this hearing record but is on file with the Subcommittee, and can also be accessed at:

   http://docs.house.gov/Committee/Calendar/ByEvent.aspx?EventID=105369

time she uses raising the funds, she risks delays and a more difficult abortion.

If that does not work, she may, in desperation, decide to seek a dangerous illegal abortion from an untrained or unlicensed practitioner. And if she cannot find the funds at all and goes on to give birth, she stands a greater chance of slipping deeper into poverty, finding no way out.

Even though all American women have the constitutional right to an abortion, the Hyde amendment is a law that objectively stops low-income women from being able to exercise their full rights.

We must ensure that every American woman can access their constitutional right to an abortion. We must end the Hyde amendment.

Now, there are 15 States that have done this with a policy to cover abortion with State funds and who do so in practice. Women in these States are so fortunate because they can actually make decisions over their own lives. Unfortunately, this leaves the women who live in the rest of the 35 States with no alternative.

But there is a bill in Congress that remedies this situation. Congresswoman Barbara Lee is the author of the EACH Woman Act. Her bill would ensure that abortion coverage is available not just for wealthy women, but for all women. Her bill would ensure that the constitutional rights of all women are upheld.

I am proud to be a cosponsor of this bill and to be one of 120 cosponsors of this bill in the House of Representatives, all of whom believe that it is time for the Hyde amendment to end.

And I would like to ask Kierra Johnson two questions. For one thing, there was a witness who said that the public supports the Hyde Amendment; however, it is my understanding that the public agrees that the Hyde amendment should end and that a woman should be able to determine her access to health care and abortion services. That is question number one.

My other question is, under the Hyde amendment, States are permitted to use their own funds to provide abortion coverage to Medicaid recipients. Of course, 15 States have chosen to do this. Do you find that in these States that use their own funds women have overall better healthcare outcomes because of better access to family planning?

Ms. JOHNSON. Thank you, Congresswoman.

It is true, the majority of Americans support the lifting of abortion bans, including the Hyde amendment, and they support that Medicaid cover a full range of pregnancy options, including abortion services.

And when women have access to abortion, when they can afford abortion, the quality of life of women and their families improves. Studies are showing that.

A woman who seeks an abortion but is denied is more likely to fall in poverty than one who obtains one. And I mentioned earlier in my testimony that the burden does fall hard on low-income women. Restrictions on Medicaid coverage of abortion forces one in four women, poor women, seeking an abortion to carry an unwanted pregnancy to term. This also compounds other health disparities facing women of color and low-income women of color across the Nation.

And so the short answer is, yes, we do see improved quality of life for women, but not just women, for their families and for their children and for their communities.

Ms. CHU. Thank you.

I yield back.

Mr. FRANKS. I thank the gentlelady.

And I would now yield to Mr. King from Iowa for 5 minutes.

Mr. KING. Thank you, Mr. Chairman.

I thank the witnesses for your testimony.

I would start with, as I listened to Mr. Cohen's opening remarks, he said that, "Women have an undisputed right to abortion." And that caught my ear, because I dispute that. I dispute the decision of *Roe v. Wade* and *Doe v. Bolton*. I dispute the rationale that they contrived to or arrive at the decision that I think was preconceived, and then they created the legal rationale to get to their conclusion.

And one of the rebuttals that I would offer for such a thing is that we know this: America was founded on the concept that our rights come from God. And when our rights come from God, how would it be possible that those rights could confer a right to kill a baby?

And so I pose that question for deliberation, and I hope a lot of people across this country begin to think about the sacred nature of human life and about the moment that life begins.

This right to choose being well settled is also a component of that opening statement, with which I disagree. It is not well settled. It has been a fight for 43 years, and it will be a fight until it is over. But what we are seeing is for the ultrasound, science expanding, watching babies move, burp, laugh, react to outside stimuli in the womb, the personalities that one can discern by seeing the ultrasound.

I have a staff person in my Sioux City office, and I will give you his name. He is State Senator Bill Anderson. On his bookcase, he has framed the ultrasound of his first born. And he knew he was a father when he saw that.

I would turn, first, to Ms. Plaster. And you gave us some valuable data, I believe. And some of this data—I would ask this question, of the roughly—and I don't remember the name—the number you gave us, but roughly 60 million abortions have been committed in this country since *Roe v. Wade* or in that zone. If you have a more precise number, I am happy to hear it. But I wanted to ask you, what percentage of those abortions were Black babies?

Ms. PLASTER. Thank you for the question, Congressman.

I do think I have a more—I think it is closer to about 55, 56 million abortions now since *Roe v. Wade* was decided.

And to your question about how many of those, I can't say that I have it in front of me at this moment, but I would be happy to look that up and provide it to the Subcommittee.

Mr. KING. I would ask you to enter into the record if you would provide that information to this Committee.

Ms. PLASTER. I will.

Mr. KING. Thank you. And how soon do you think you can do that.

Ms. PLASTER. Today.

Mr. KING. That would be excellent.

And would your estimation be that if the Black population is 12 to 13 percent of the overall U.S. population, would you expect that that percentage of Black abortions would be greater or lesser than the representation in the overall population?

Ms. PLASTER. Thank you. Studies have shown that it is greater, according to the CDC. And the Guttmacher Institute has even more accurate information, because the abortion centers give their information directly to Guttmacher. Many States do not have a mandatory law to submit abortion records to the CDC or their State health department. So according to Guttmacher, yes, it is, African Americans are disproportionately represented in the abortion.

Mr. KING. Would you have any idea why that is not being called genocide by the Black community?

Ms. PLASTER. Thankfully, I know that there are good pro-life organizations that—good pro-life Black organizations that are calling attention to this. And I know that, for instance, Ryan Bomberger has done a great job in calling attention to this as genocide.

Mr. KING. Thank you.

Ms. Johnson, if one were to be there at the delivery of a litter of puppies, and as a puppy was partially delivered took a device and either crushed the skull or sucked the brains out of that baby, would you be committing a crime in most States?

Ms. JOHNSON. I couldn't speak to what is considered a crime with puppies.

Mr. KING. If I asked you to research that and come back to this panel with a response in the fashion that Ms. Plaster has promised, could you do that? Would you do that? I know you could do that. Would you?

Ms. JOHNSON. I could, and I could also talk to you about the research and the anecdotal information I have about Black communities.

Mr. KING. And I think that is valuable information. Not the subject of this hearing.

Ms. JOHNSON. I would love to talk about Black communities if you would like me to.

Mr. KING. But I am asking you a specific question. Would you deliver that information to me? I have asked you if you believe that would be committing a crime in the several States. And I am going to ask you to answer this formally back to this Committee.

But I would tell you the answer, and the answer is, yes, it would be. And the contrast is that as it stands, as you are advocating, you cannot do to a puppy what is now currently legal to do in America to a baby created in the image of God, and that is the center of this topic here today.

I thank all the witnesses, and I yield back the balance of my time.

Mr. FRANKS. I thank the gentleman.

And I would now yield to the Ranking Member of the full Committee, Mr. Conyers.

Mr. CONYERS. Thank you, Mr. Chairman.

This has been a fascinating subject here that I didn't realize was so emotional to so many people both on the panel and in the audience.

But let's start with you, Ms. Johnson. I want to begin by asking you just to go over the impact that you think women of color receive and are affected by the Hyde amendment itself. Could you do that for me?

Ms. JOHNSON. Certainly. Thank you, Congressman.

Women of color, young women, low-income women are disproportionately affected by the Hyde amendment. The reality is that healthcare disparities exist for women of color, for people of color, across healthcare issues, and reproductive health is no different. A lack of health insurance, a lack of affordability of health care, meaning a lack of an ability to even think about paying out-of-pocket, a lack of sexual health information, a lack of access to contraceptive services, in addition to stigma and shame, right, compounds these issues.

And that means higher rates of unintended pregnancy for women of color, which means we have to make sure that a full range of options, including abortion, are accessible, because when they are not, particularly for low-income women of color, there is a greater chance of them falling further and deeper in poverty.

Mr. CONYERS. Thank you. Does the Hyde amendment, in your view, affect the quality of health care that low-income women receive?

Ms. JOHNSON. The Hyde amendment prevents women from even being able to make a decision about their health care. So, yes. I mean, that alone, not being able to access, right, economically access the decision that you have made, the health care that you have chosen, of course that impacts the quality of health care.

We just heard about how does this affect Black women and Black families and Black communities. The reality is that we cannot possibly think that helping Black women is going to happen by taking yet another opportunity to take decisionmaking away from them. That is not the way for us to support and respect Black women and Black families.

Women of color want more access to health care, not more barriers to health care. They want more child care and affordable options of child care. Women want, particularly Black women, an answer to the high maternity mortality rates in our communities.

And so the Hyde amendment means adding, right, it means providing a full range of options for women so that women can make the best decisions for their health care.

Mr. CONYERS. Thank you.

My last question is how do you think legislators, we in Washington, are we best positioned to make decisions about a woman's health and well-being, and how do we get better at it?

Ms. JOHNSON. Abortion can be a complex issue, and people have opinions. People have feelings. People have thoughts. But however we feel about abortion, we should not deny poor women access to it because they are poor.

So as legislators, creating ways that give decisionmaking back to women is a positive step forward. And the decisionmaking around reproductive health and rights issues, right, when we are making decisions about whether to be pregnant and whether to parent, give us the space and opportunity to be able to do that with our doctors, with our loved ones, with our families, and in the context of the situations and circumstances we are in.

Mr. CONYERS. Thank you very much for your responses and for being with us at this hearing. I think this is one of the ways that we will become more thoughtful about the complexity of abortion and what it means to low-income women. Thank you so very much.

Ms. JOHNSON. Thank you.

Mr. CONYERS. And I yield back, Mr. Chairman.

Mr. FRANKS. I thank the gentleman.

And I now recognize the gentleman from Texas, Mr. Gohmert.

Mr. GOHMERT. Thank you, Mr. Chairman.

I won't be cheering today or clapping when I hear that, basically, the propaganda campaign that Margaret Sanger started, because she believed, she knew in her heart we will be better off if women who are poor and women of color are encouraged, pushed to have abortions, basically convince them to have genocide. It has worked. Of course, it disproportionately affects women of color and poor women. That is the design of abortion. That is the design of eugenics.

And I would like to yield the rest of my time for a video.

[video shown.]

Mr. GOHMERT. I yield back.

Mr. FRANKS. I thank the gentleman.

I am going to recognize myself now for 5 minutes for questions.

I have had both the privilege and the burden of dealing with this issue for a very long time, because a long time ago I came to a very stark realization that these were really babies. And if I believed that we are all created equal, if I believed that every child is a child of God, if I believed that every child was important, then it became important to me to try to do what was possible to live out that ideal of the Founding Fathers that we hold these truths to be self-evident, that we are all created equal and that every person would have a chance to live.

EDTR ROSEN

Mr. FRANKS. And I don't know how this debate has developed the way it has where Americans seem to be so at each other, because we have been here before. You know, a lot of times, my friends on the left, they attack us for using the example of Dred Scott. The reason that it is used so often is because it is so profoundly parallel. The Supreme Court comes along and says, the African American slave is not a person. And there were those who believed that wasn't true. There were those that believed that this was a human being worthy of protection, and they stood up and did everything that they could to do that, to change that. And, finally, we changed.

And now we look back, and there is not too many people that would argue that case anymore. They see the personhood. And sometimes when we finally see the humanity of the victim and the inhumanity of what is being done to them, somehow it begins to dawn on you.

And I—I pray that somehow when we are talking about born-alive children, that a light goes on. That we realize if we are not going to protect born-alive babies, then we have allowed ourselves to be dragged into that Samarian night where the light of human compassion has gone out, and the survival of the fitness has prevailed over humanity. And I pray that day has not come to America.

And I heard a testimony today that gave me great hope, because, Ms. Jessen, you are living proof that when babies survive abortion, they go on to bring a loving, noble message to humanity. And I just—I know you have said some things to our Committee here, but I would just ask if you have anything else that you would like to tell America regarding the protection of babies born alive that have survived abortion?

Ms. JESSEN. Thank you, Congressman. I would like to thank you for being such a man of such great courage.

And I would—I have been listening in the hearing today, after speaking, after explaining that I lived through an abortion. Often, when I am in the midst of abortion advocates, they never can answer this one question, and it is this: If abortion was merely about—is merely about women's rights, then what were mine? And I have been listening to the great round of applause for the ending the lives of these children, but these very same people behind me applauding, I would like to tell you that if need be, I would lay my life down for you, because no greater love has a man than this, than to lay down his life for his friend. And so as I listen to you applaud for—for—for death, I want to tell you how valuable you are.

And to America, I would say this, wake up. And, you know, we are so worried about every single other issue under the sun, and we—we don't talk about this one. We are embarrassed by the social issues. We are embarrassed by the people that love God, and we are embarrassed by defending the most vulnerable among us, and we wonder why we have people killing each other. We have got our priorities wrong. We have abandoned God. We are embarrassed by him, and we will not remain free without him.

So I would call on my Nation to repent. What a word. We don't say that anymore. But I would call on my Nation to have—to—that God would wake us up. And—and—yeah. That is what I would say. I don't feel it was quite articulate, but here you are.

Mr. FRANKS. Your message is heard in the context of your life, my lady.

I would like now to begin a second round of questions.

And I would recognize the gentleman from Texas, Mr. Gohmert, for 5 minutes.

Mr. GOHMERT. Thank you. And I appreciate our witnesses being here, and I mean all of them. It is important that people have a chance to speak what they believe.

As a former attorney and judge and chief justice, I look at the way the law in America has developed. Most of us think the Dred Scott decision was perhaps the worst decision in American history. How in the world could people prevail before our highest court in the land by saying these slaves are my property. I paid for them. I own them. The U.S. Government has no right whatsoever to tell me what I can do with my own property any more than they can tell me what I can do with my own body. It is my right to own another person. And the Supreme Court, to their great shame, said that is right. This is your property. The U.S. Government has no right to interfere with what you choose to do with your property.

51

I would encourage, Mr. Chairman, people who think Margaret
Sanger was a hero, to go back and look at the things that she advocated in the way of eugenics. She believed that people who were
poor, people of color, were genetically flawed and, therefore, it was
a good thing to push them to have abortions. And if they couldn't
be convinced, then, you know, forcibly sterilize them, because we
need to be moving toward a higher plain of human being, not real-
izing that by what she advocated, she was bringing humanity down
to the lowest possible level, the level of the animal kingdom where
you can kill or destroy if it suits you.

So we have heard about the inappropriate intervention into
healthcare decisions. And I struggle with the disparity in the argu-
ment that says no one should ever inappropriately intervene in a
healthcare decision on behalf of a woman, and yet, we will tell that
same woman later in life, Sorry, under ObamaCare, if you are too
old to get a pacemaker—as the President himself said, you are better off just saying take a pain pill. You don't get a pacemaker.
There seems to be a disparity in thinking that you—we would advocate you can't intervene and say the life you are carrying, if delivered alive, even if you are trying to destroy that life, or as the
doctor indicated for late-term abortions, you pull one leg off then
you pull the other leg off then you pull the arm off then you pull
the other arm off. And as you have heard him describe before, you
reach in with the clamps for something bulbous, and you know you
have the skull. You rip that off.

And as Mr. King was trying to point out, anybody who does those
things to a puppy, everybody in the country would be demanding
they go to prison. But we have elevated this procedure to such a
high level that the highest court in the land could say, Hey, that
baby is your property. You can do whatever you want with it.

So I won't be cheering today. I will remain broken hearted for
my country and for the success Margaret Sanger has had in advocating for eugenics and genocide and this country's participation in
what she hoped to achieve.

I yield back.

Mr. FRANKS. And I thank the gentleman.

And I now yield to Mr. Conyers.

Mr. CONYERS. Thank you, Mr. Chairman.

This has been an unusual hearing in a number of respects, but
I would like to ask Ms. Johnson just one question, because over the
past several years, there have been a marked increase in the number of States passing targeted regulations for abortion providers
making it practically impossible, certainly a lot, lot more difficult
for safe abortions to occur and other legislative measures designed
to impede women's safe and legal medical care.

Can you discuss the impact, in your view, that such laws have
had on low-income women?

Ms. JOHNSON. Thank you, Congressman, for your question.

You are right, there are trap laws. Women have to often travel
hundreds of miles because over 89 percent of counties don't have
an abortion provider. There are also waiting periods which force
women to wait additional days after they have already made a
choice in health care.

And the Hyde amendment exacerbates the barriers that already exist for low-income women or any woman who is seeking abortion services.

It is interesting that we are bringing up slavery in this space. When you own somebody's decisionmaking, you own them. When you get to decide for them whether or not their body has value, you own them. When you decide they are valuable as black or not, you actually don't get to make that decision. We are valuable, and women are valuable.

The Hyde amendment simply says set us free. We are not simple minded. We are not being duped. Women are choosing to be pregnant and have children. The majority of women who have abortion are parents. They care. They care about their families.

The Hyde amendment is about increasing coverage of insurance. It is about returning decisionmaking back to women. It is about setting us free.

Mr. CONYERS. Do you think we should consider repealing the Hyde amendment or move forward with other legislation since— since we are closing out this subject?

Ms. JOHNSON. Yes. We should repeal the Hyde amendment. There are a lot of support from the American people.

As a matter of fact, there's strong support among millennials, among African Americans, and Latino voters in particular, with millennials supporting the EACH Woman Act at 66 percent; African American supporting at 68 percent, and Latinos supporting at 55 percent. So, yes, I think we need to repeal the Hyde amendment. And I think we need to pass the EACH Woman Act, and the American people agree.

Mr. CONYERS. Thank you so much.

And I thank you, Mr. Chairman.

Mr. FRANKS. And I thank the gentleman. And I will now yield to myself for 5 minutes.

Ms. Grossu, I will begin with you. Will you, please, talk about the ironic juxtaposition between the amount of medical care available to a premature baby who is wanted and a live premature baby who is as a result of an abortion and deemed unwanted.

Ms. GROSSU. Thank you, Mr. Chairman, for sure.

I would, first, like to make the distinction too that abortion is not health care. Killing your own child is not health care, and American taxpayers should not be funding this. And there is no such thing as a safe abortion either. Abortion is a very dangerous procedure. Having said that, I will go to your—your question.

Essentially, a premature baby now can survive at 20 weeks post realization if given proper care and treatment, is—is able to make it. And this kind of care is being held in an incubator or being given oxygen using a little infant oxygen mask, even being kept warm to maintain body temperature of the baby. These types of treatments are given to babies because a woman decides that she wants that child. So that child's value is dependent on a person— another person's opinion of that child.

So if the woman wants her child, that baby is going to be given the absolute best care that our medical communities have. And if that woman deems that she does not want that child, that child is thrown in the trash, as we have seen time and time again, as Jill

53

Stanek has expressed, as the videos—we have seen the videos that the child is taken apart and the baby's body parts are being sold on the market.

And so we are asking under this born-alive bill, that abortionists be required to give basic immediate care to a baby once that baby has taken his or her first breath. This—these are children who are outside of the vaginal canal. They are recognized as legal persons under our laws, and they should be protected.

Mr. FRANKS. Well, thank you, Ms. Grossu.

You know, I think that is—the profundity of all of this at times for me is that somehow, how do we separate the wanted child from the unwanted child. It occurs to me that if we say that that child is unwanted, that we say nothing about the child. We say only about something about those of us around the child.

And if, indeed, we have come to the point where what gives a child the right to live and the right to protection is being wanted or unwanted, then all the dreams of the Founding Fathers are lost, and all of the things that those people out in Arlington National Cemetery died to preserve are lost. Because America's founding dream was this notion that all of us were created equal and these were rights given by God that this thing was a miracle, and that to secure that right, that is the reason governments came about. And that it had its power from consent of the government.

You know, there is no way to articulate the tragedy of even losing even one little child. But I would suggest to you that something else is lost here, and that is it is not the dying that leaves scars, it is the killing. And when we create this stone in our hearts and in our conscious to where we are able to say this born-alive child is only protectable if they are wanted.

Do you understand where we have come to as Americans? Do you understand what's left? If we don't want to protect a born-alive child, then who—who should we protect? If killing a born-alive child is not wrong, then on what basis do we say anything is wrong? What protection do any of us have when, as a society, we harden our hearts to the extent that we will stand by and advocate and say it is a right to kill a born-alive child, and there should be no protection for that child?

I do fear for my country. And I pray that somehow in the days ahead, that our country will begin to consider who we are. I would call upon Donald Trump to say who he is on this issue on born-alive protection. I would call on Hillary Clinton to do the same thing. I would call on the U.S. Senate to bring this bill up for a vote. Because if—if we are no longer committed to protecting born-alive children, then it is time to board the place up that we are in and go home, because the battle is lost. And this ideal that all of us were created equal and are children of God have slipped from us. And I for one do not believe that.

I believe that Americans are still protectors of children. I believe that America's best days are still ahead. And I believe that some of the testimony we have had here today is the most compelling that I have heard in a long time.

And I would just say to those of you that disagree, there is no hate in my heart toward you. But I would also say to something that William Wilberforce said a long time. He said—and he was talking about slavery. He said, you can turn away, but you can never again say that you did not know. Today, you know that born-alive children are dying, and there are those of us trying to protect them. And I only pray that somehow that as it has happened somehow in the past in America, that we come to the conclusion that, you know what, this is not who we are, and we still hold these truths to be self-evident, that we are all created, and that makes us a miracle, and that is worth protecting.

So thank you, all, for coming today. That concludes this Committee hearing.

And I have a little script here. Without objection, all Members will have 5 legislative days to submit additional requests for the witnesses for additional materials for the record.

And with that, God bless you all. This hearing is adjourned.

[Whereupon, at 10:53 a.m., the Subcommittee was adjourned.]

APPENDIX

MATERIAL SUBMITTED FOR THE HEARING RECORD

Response to Hearing Question from Genevieve Plaster, M.A.,
Senior Policy Analyst, Charlotte Lozier Institute

House Committee on the Judiciary, Subcommittee on the Constitution and Civil Justice
Hearing on "The Ultimate Civil Right: Examining the Hyde Amendment and the Born Alive
Infants Protection Act"
September 23, 2016
Genevieve Plaster, Charlotte Lozier Institute

Answer to a question from Congressman King regarding how many abortions are performed for
African Americans:

Two entities collect national abortion reporting data: the Centers for Disease Control (CDC)
and the Guttmacher Institute. Regarding how many abortions are performed annually on African
American women and their unborn children, the CDC reports this to be ***148,971 or 27.8 percent***
of all reported abortions. *The Census Bureau reports that the African American community*
represents 13.3 percent of the population.[1] As such, ***the rate of abortion for African Americans***
is more than twice their representation in the U.S. population.

According to the latest CDC abortion surveillance report (data from 2012)[2]:

- "**non-Hispanic black women had the highest abortion rate (27.8** abortions per 1,000 women aged 15–44 years)";
- "Among the 27 areas that reported cross-classified race/ethnicity data for 2012 (Table 12) non-Hispanic white women and **non-Hispanic black women** accounted for the largest percentages of abortions (37.6% and **36.7%, respectively)**";
- "for abortions among **unmarried women, the percentage was higher for non-Hispanic black women (91.1%)** than for non-Hispanic white (82.9%) or Hispanic women (83.9%)

The Guttmacher Institute obtains abortion survey data directly from abortion providers, including those
with which it was formerly affiliated as the research arm of Planned Parenthood.[3] According to its latest
abortion report (data from 2014)[4]:

- "28% [of all women obtaining abortions] were black";
- "black women were substantially overrepresented"

---

[1] This does not include data for African American bi-racial individuals.
https://www.census.gov/quickfacts/table/PST045215/00
[2] "During the period covered by this report, the total annual number of abortions reported to CDC was consistently
approximately 70% of the number recorded by the Guttmacher Institute which uses numerous active follow-up
techniques to increase the completeness of the data obtained through its periodic national census of abortion providers. Although
most reporting areas collect and send abortion data to CDC, this information is submitted to CDC voluntarily. Consequently,
during 2003–2012, five of the 52 reporting areas did not provide CDC data on a consistent annual basis, and for 2012, CDC did
not obtain any information from California, Maryland, or New Hampshire." See
http://www.cdc.gov/mmwr/preview/mmwrhtml/ss6410a1.htm
[3] Donovan, Chuck and Nora Sullivan. Abortion Reporting: Tears in the Fabric, December 2012, accessed at:
https://lozierinstitute.org/wp-content/uploads/2012/12/American-Report-Series-ABORTION-REPORTING-LAWS-
Dec-12-Update-1-13.pdf. An updated paper ranking states' abortion reporting systems may be found at:
https://lozierinstitute.org/abortion-reporting-toward-a-better-national-standard-summary/
[4] https://www.guttmacher.org/sites/default/files/report_pdf/characteristics-us-abortion-patients-2014.pdf

Letter from Melissa Ohden, Founder, The Abortion Survivors Network

September 19, 2016

To: Chairman Franks

The House of Representatives Constitution SubCommittee Members

Life is the ultimate civil right.

Our Federal government plays an important role in protecting the lives of it's citizens, this ultimate civil right, including those who are not yet born. The Hyde Amendment and the Born Alive Infants Protection Act are two important facets to protecting these lives.

The Constitution recognizes the most fundamental principle: human equality and the protection of one's right to life. Regardless of age, size, stage of development or dependency on another human being, the Constitution requires that EVERY human life be protected.

As you are aware, the Hyde Amendment bars the use of certain Federal funds to pay for abortion except in certain circumstances. September 30th, 2016, is the fortieth anniversary of the Hyde Amendment. According to a 2010 statement from the Center for Reproductive Rights, the Hyde amendment has prevented over a million abortions. As an abortion rights group, they call this "prevention of abortion." As someone who values life and the Constitution, I call this protecting over a million lives from the death of abortion.

#HelloHyde, (a social media campaign that puts a face to the amendment and its' positive impact on American's lives), spokeswoman Gina Mallica recently stated, *"Low income children deserve a chance at life, not a government subsidized death."*

I couldn't agree more with Ms. Mallica. *It is unjust to deny any unborn child's right to life*, and when we recognize that socioeconomic reasons are frequently cited by women as the reason for their abortion (according to the Guttmacher Institute in 2005, 73% of women identified not being able to afford a baby now, while 74% cited that having a child would interfere with their education, work or ability to care for dependents), one can see just how important the Hyde Amendment is for the protection of all American lives, especially those who are most vulnerable to death by abortion due to socioeconomic circumstances.

I am not writing today about constitutional law or as an expert in the Hyde Amendment and abortion, however.

I am writing today *to put a face to the civil right of life*, to what late term abortion looks like and to the importance of infants born alive after abortion being provided timely and appropriate medical care.

In August of 1977, my biological mother, a 19-year-old college student, was forced to undergo a saline infusion abortion. My medical records from St. Luke's Hospital in Sioux City, Iowa, indicate that she was believed to be approximately 20 weeks pregnant with me at that time. They state that "a saline infusion for an abortion was done, but was unsuccessful." Those same records then proceed to later identify a complication of her pregnancy as "saline infusion."

A saline infusion abortion involves injecting a toxic salt solution into the amniotic fluid surrounding the preborn child in the womb. The intent of that toxic salt solution is to slowly scald the child to death, from the outside in. If you read about it online or in medical journals, you will find children like me called the "red skinned," or "candy-apple babies," because that toxic solution would turn the skin bright red, as it peeled it away and moved internally into the organs.

This abortion procedure typically lasted about three days--72 hours. The child soaked in that toxic salt solution until their life was effectively ended and then premature labor was induced, with the intent of that deceased child being delivered.

In my own case, I didn't soak in that toxic salt solution for just three days. My medical records indicate that I soaked in it for five. For five days, I soaked in that toxic salt solution while multiple attempts were made to induce my biological mother's labor with me to expel my dead body. Finally, on the fifth day of the abortion procedure, her labor was successfully induced. I should have been delivered dead that day as a "successful" abortion, a deceased child. But by the grace of God, I was born alive.

I can't even begin to imagine the horrible pain and suffering that I experienced during those five days of the abortion procedure and in the days and weeks that followed. Abortion doesn't spare a child from suffering, it causes suffering.

I weighed a little less than 3 pounds (2 pounds, 14 ounces), when I was delivered at St. Luke's Hospital in Sioux City, Iowa, in that final step of the abortion procedure, which indicated to the medical professionals that my birthmother was much further along in her pregnancy than she had realized and the abortionist failed to admit to. In fact, one of the first notations in my medical records states that I looked like I was about 31 weeks gestational age when I survived. Sadly, whether I was 31 weeks or 20 weeks, what happened to me was permitted by Federal law.

The fight for my life was far from over after I was delivered in this failed abortion.

In 2013, I learned through contact with my biological mother's family (who I am incredibly thankful to have in my life, along with members of my biological father's family) that not only was this abortion forced upon her against her will, but also that it was my maternal grandmother, a nurse, who delivered me in this final step of the abortion procedure.

Unfortunately, I also learned that when my grandmother realized that the abortion had not succeeded in ending my life, she demanded that I be left to die.

I may never know how, exactly, two nurses who were on staff that day found out about me (one of whom has had their story passed down to my adoptive parents) or where they found me, but what I do know is that their willingness to fight for medical care to be provided to me saved my life.

I know where children like me were left to die at St. Luke's Hospital—a utility closet. In 2014, I met a nurse who assisted in a saline infusion abortion there in 1976, and delivered a living baby boy. After he was delivered alive, she followed her superior's orders and placed him in the utility closet in a bucket of formaldehyde to be picked up later as medical waste after he died there, alone.

A bucket of formaldehyde in a utility closet was meant to be my fate after I wasn't first scalded to death through the abortion.

Yet I am alive today because I was ultimately given the medical care that I so desperately needed and deserved.

I am thankful that the abortion meant to end my life actually occurred at a hospital, as the medical treatment that I needed for my severe respiratory and liver problems and seizures--the oxygen, blood transfusions and everything thereafter was located right there.

If my birthmother's abortion would have occurred at an abortion clinic, I truly believe that I would not be alive today. The medical care would have been long in coming to me, if at all.

To say that I am grateful to be alive would be an understatement. No, we may never know if I made it all the way to that utility closet and the bucket of formaldehyde or I was simply laid aside, but the truth about the location of where I was left will never change the truth of the intent of why I was left. I was meant to be killed in the abortion and then when that didn't succeed, I was left to die.

As a fellow American, as a fellow human being, I deserved the same right to life, the same equal protection under the law as each and every one of you. Yet we know that our great nation falls terribly short when it comes to protecting the most vulnerable of its' citizens.

We live in a day and time where the science of human development, the power of ultrasound, and the sheer number of survivors like me (I know of 209 others just like me through my work as the founder of The Abortion Survivors Network, although I am sure the actual number is much higher) clearly shows the truth about life. There should no longer be a question of when life begins. *There should no longer be the question of which lives, if any, should be protected.*

Every child should be protected regardless of the circumstances of how they were conceived or what the expectations are for what their life will look like.

The question that does remain, however, is what you will do in the face of this reality about life and abortion in our nation.

I am writing today as one among tens of millions of children who have been impacted by abortion to ask you: Will you ensure that the Hyde Amendment remain in place? Will you ensure that children like me who survive abortions are assured proper and timely medical care when we are lucky enough to survive an abortion? Will you protect the ultimate human right—the right to life?

Sincerely,

Melissa Ohden

Founder, The Abortion Survivors Network

Prepared Statement of the Honorable Bob Goodlatte, a Representative in Congress from the State of Virginia, and Chairman, Committee on the Judiciary

Statement of Judiciary Chairman Bob Goodlatte
House Constitution Subcommittee Hearing on
The Ultimate Civil Right: Examining the Hyde Amendment
and the Born Alive Infants Protection Act
September 23, 2016

I'm pleased to see that one of the greatest pro-life leaders in Congress, Trent Franks, is holding this hearing today on the anniversaries of the House passage of the Born-Alive Abortion Survivors Protection Act and the enactment of the first Hyde Amendment.

The Born-Alive Abortion Survivors Protection Act is simple, yet profound, insofar as it might be a reflection of the nation's conscience. Its operative provisions provide that in the case of an abortion or attempted abortion that results in a child born alive, any health care practitioner present must exercise the same degree of professional care to preserve the life of the child as he or she would render to any other child born alive at the same gestational age.

Babies are born alive during failed abortions. The House Judiciary Committee, just last year, heard direct testimony by two grown women who, as babies, survived attempted abortions. The mother of one of them, Gianna Jessen, was advised by Planned Parenthood to have an abortion. But as Ms. Jessen testified: "Instead of dying, after 18 hours of being burned in my mother's womb, I was delivered alive in an abortion clinic in Los Angeles on April 6, 1977." Her medical records state clearly that she was "born alive" during an abortion. She continued, "Thankfully, the abortionist was not at work yet. Had he been there, he would have ended my life with strangulation, suffocation, or leaving me there to die. Instead, a nurse called an ambulance, and I was rushed to a hospital. Doctors did not expect me to live. I did. I was later diagnosed with Cerebral Palsy, which was caused by a lack of oxygen to my brain while surviving the abortion. I was never supposed to hold my head up or walk. I do. And Cerebral Palsy is a great gift to me."

Just think of that for a moment. Ms. Jessen says cerebral palsy is a gift to her <u>because it came with the gift of life</u>. She forgave her mother long ago, and gives praise each day for that gift of life, which she enjoys to its fullest to this day.

The Born-Alive Abortion Survivors Protection Act is now in the hands of the Senate. I ask all Senators today to see the body of a baby, on the floor, born alive during a failed abortion. I ask that they see the humanity of that small baby, and vote to bring that baby to a hospital where she belongs -- and not leave her with the abortionist.

Finally, however stark Americans' differences of opinion can be on the matter of abortion generally, there has been long, bipartisan agreement that federal taxpayer funds should not be used to destroy innocent life. The Hyde Amendment, named for its chief sponsor, former House Judiciary Committee Chairman Henry Hyde, has prohibited the federal funding of abortions since 1976, when it passed a House and Senate that was composed overwhelmingly of Democratic Members. It has been renewed each appropriations cycle with few changes for over 35 years, supported by Congresses controlled by both parties, and Presidents from both parties. The Congressional Budget Office has estimated that the Hyde Amendment has led to as many as 675,000 fewer abortions each year. Let that sink in for a few precious moments. The policy we will be discussing today has likely given America the gift of millions more children, and consequently many more mothers and fathers who have had many more children of their own. What a stunningly wondrous legacy.

I look forward to hearing from all our witnesses today.

www.ingramcontent.com/pod-product-compliance
Lightning Source LLC
Chambersburg PA
CBHW081414280526
45788CB00009B/3104